M000232684

FIELD GUIDE TO MODERN

Diesel
Locomotives

GREG McDONNELL

© 2002 Greg McDonnell. All rights reserved.
This book may not be reproduced in part or in whole without written permission of the publisher, except in the case of brief quotations used in reviews. Published by Kalmbach Publishing Co., 21027 Crossroads Circle, Waukesha, WI 53187.

Printed in Canada.

02 03 04 05 06 07 08 09 10 11   10 9 8 7 6 5 4 3 2 1

Visit our website at http://www.kalmbachbooks.com
Secure online ordering available

Publisher's Cataloging-in-Publication

McDonnell, Greg, 1954-
    Field guide to modern diesel locomotives /
    Greg McDonnell. – 1st ed.
    p.   cm.
    ISBN 0-89024-607-6

    1. Diesel locomotives. I. Title.

TJ619.M33 2002   625.26'6   QBI02-200083

Text editor: Kathleen Fraser
Research assistance: William D. Miller, Sean Graham White
Technical assistance and review: Mike Iden, Robert Lambrecht
Photos by author unless credited otherwise.

Cover and book design: Chris McCorkindale and Sue Breen
                    McCorkindale Advertising & Design

Author's Note

"Toxic model syndrome." That's how a senior motive power official with Union Pacific sums up the complex—and often confusing—model designations that builders have assigned to many contemporary locomotives. To simplify matters, UP and other roads have devised their own abbreviated designations, distilling such cumbersome terminology as SD90MAC-H, Dash 9-44CW and AC6000CW to more manageable nomenclature, such as SD90AC, C44-9 and C60AC.

For the same reason, *Trains* magazine condenses many of the more awkward model designations to simplified terminology similar to that employed by UP. However, as a reference manual, this work generally adheres to the formal model designation established by the locomotive builders and found on locomotive builder's plates, in operating manuals and other builder literature.

All weights and measurements given are nominal figures provided by the builders and/or railroads. Statistics for individual units and orders may vary.

Cover photos

Left: EMD 16-265H prime mover, UP SD90MAC-H 8202

Center: UP AC4400CW 7154 and BNSF Dash 9-44CW 4413 ready to ship at GE Erie, Pa., April 28, 1999.

Right: Amtrak-California F59PHI 2006 hurries through Escalon, Calif., with a northbound *San Joaquin* on March 12, 2000.

Contents

Storming through Keenbrook, Calif., an eastbound BNSF intermodal train makes a run for Cajon Pass on March 30, 2001. The passage of the train, with a mixed bag of motive power in a multi-colored hue, prompts the perennial question: What are all these diesels? The answer can be found within these pages. For the record, the power here consists of BNSF Dash 9-44CW 5444, BN C30-7 5588, BNSF SD45-2 6452 and BNSF SD75I 8260.

What Are All These Diesels?

T he headline appeared on a full-page ad in the February 1967 issue of *Trains* magazine, and with it, a photograph and a promise. The photograph was a memorable Don Wood image of Pennsylvania Railroad Alcos, Baldwins, EMD's and F-M's of every imaginable shape and size crowding the shop tracks in Altoona, Pa. The promise? "Just a glance through the all-new *Diesel Spotter's Guide* and you'll know their makers, model numbers, wheel arrangements, and horsepower." The first all-encompassing guide to North American diesels, Jerry A. Pinkepank's 304-page manual was, for diesel fans, just what the doctor ordered.

For a kid in school, filling the prescription was another matter. Money was always in short supply, and there were Beatle albums to buy, and 45s, and film and *Trains* magazine. It was a big day when the package marked with a Kalmbach

Railroading remains as exciting as ever, and the fascination of locomotives is undiminished. Santa Fe SD75M 211 and Dash 9-44CW 647 grind upgrade at Monolith, Calif., just after dawn on April 4, 1997.

Amtrak 200 and 415, the first and last units of its famed F40PH fleet, speed through Edgerton, Ind., with No. 30, the *Capitol Limited*, on June 27, 1992.

"K" and a 1027 North 7th Street return address arrived in the mail. Pinkepank made good on the publisher's promise. In the pulp pages behind a glossy color cover adorned with the faces of SOO GP35 722, L&N C420 1306 and Santa Fe U28CG 358, the *Diesel Spotter's Guide* told all, from the oft-disputed difference between a GP7 and a GP9, to a detailed description of the Alco Blunt truck, to spotting details and production totals for everything from the Baldwin AS16 to the GE U50. It was the best $3.50 I ever spent.

Thirty-five years and a half-dozen editions of the *Spotter's Guide* later,

locomotives and railroading have changed immeasurably. The three units that graced the cover of the original DSG have long ago been scrapped and the railroads that owned them have been swallowed up in mergers; GE, still considered a newcomer in the road-diesel trade when the first *Diesel Spotter's Guide* hit the stands, has been the number-one locomotive builder in North America for nearly 20 years... and $3.50 will buy a good cup of coffee.

Railroading, nevertheless, remains as exciting as ever, and the fascination of locomotives is undiminished by the consolidation of the continent's major

railroads into a handful of super-systems. Through it all, Kalmbach and authors Jerry A. Pinkepank and Louis A. Marre have maintained the standard established in 1967 with continuously updated versions of the diesel reference book known to generations of locomotive fans as simply "the DSG."

This work picks up new locomotive production where Louis Marre's *Diesel Locomotives: The First 50 Years* (Kalmbach 1995) leaves off. However, its starting point is not a single date. Electro-Motive coverage begins with the 1972 introduction of the Dash 2 series and all models cataloged at that time. This includes the SW1000, SW1001 and SW1500, switcher models that predate the Dash 2 but remained in production beyond 1972. General Electric coverage begins with the Dash 7 Series, introduced in 1977. Wabtec's MotivePower Industries, along with its Morrison-Knudsen/MK Rail/Boise Locomotive group predecessors, which began building locomotives at Boise, Idaho, in 1991, is also included.

Although the production of MLW-Bombardier falls within the chronological coverage of this volume, the fact that none of the company's locomotives remain in service on Class 1 railroads (in fact, very few remain in service in North America at all) precludes inclusion here. Pre-1977 GE U-series "U-boat" models are excluded for the same reason. Although a small number of U-series GE's do survive in the employ of short lines, the last U-boat in service on a Class 1 railroad, CSXT U23B 3305, was retired in 2000. All of these models are, however, included in Marre's *Diesel Locomotives: The First 50 Years*.

Industrial locomotives and rebuilds are outside the realm of this book.

Generations pass. Heading up an eastbound symbol freight, Conrail B36-7 5030 blasts past brand-new Santa Fe Dash 8-40CW 836, awaiting delivery at GE's back gate in Erie, Pa., on May 8, 1992.

However, a few exceptions have been made. EMD BL20-2's, GE Super 7 locomotives and several Morrison-Knudsen/Boise Locomotive models constructed using the frame and some remanufactured components from retired locomotives are included here. While convention dictates that a locomotive is defined by its frame, the aforementioned models are essentially new locomotives constructed on a reused platform. From a trackside perspective, they fall quite squarely within the mandate of this book, and its goal to help answer that perennial question: What are all these diesels?

Almost ready to ship, BNSF Dash 9-44CW 4393 rides the transfer table between Buildings 10 and 26 at GE in Erie, Pa., on April 26, 1999.

General Electric Transportation Systems

Located on the outskirts of Erie, Pa., between CSXT's one-time New York Central Water Level Route main line and the shores of Lake Erie, General Electric Transportation System's locomotive plant is one of the most storied institutions in railroading. Opened in 1911, the 350-acre facility has been the birthplace of legions of locomotives dispatched to the four corners of the Earth.

The number-one locomotive builder in North America since 1983, General Electric was a latecomer to the domestic road-diesel market. Indeed, many railroads were already retiring—and replacing—first-generation diesels when GE introduced the U25B in 1960. The Erie builder may have been late with its first road-diesel designed for North American mainline freight duty, but the U25B was of rich pedigree.

A pioneer in electric, gas-electric and diesel-electric propulsion, GE built its first locomotive, a 30-ton, two-axle steeple-cab electric, at its works in Lynn, Mass., in 1893. Electric traction projects, including double-truck electrics built by GE's Schenectady, N.Y., works in 1895-96 for B&O's Baltimore Tunnel and the 1906 electrification of NYC lines into New York's Grand Central Terminal, were among the company's early claims to fame. However, GE also played a significant role in the advancement and success of internal-combustion power, particularly after its locomotive and traction business was relocated to the Erie works in 1911.

Early GE achievements include the 1913 construction of Dan Patch

SP AC4400CW 208

gas-electric No. 100, America's first successful internal-combustion locomotive, as well as what is regarded as the first functional diesel-electric locomotive in the United States, Jay Street Connecting No. 4, built in 1918. As a partner in the Alco-GE-Ingersoll-Rand consortium, a pioneer builder of box-cab switchers,

GE had a stake in the locomotive believed to be the first commercially successful diesel-electric in the world, Central of New Jersey No. 1000.

In addition to constructing its own locomotives and gas-cars, GE also served as a supplier of electrical and control equipment for hundreds of early gas-electrics and diesel-electrics produced by other builders, including Electro-Motive and Alco. In 1935, before the opening of La Grange, Electro-Motive contracted GE's Erie works to assemble its Winton-powered, box-cab testbeds 511-512; B&O 50, a similar locomotive delivered for passenger service on the road's famed *Royal Blue*; and Delaware, Lackawanna & Western SC-model switchers 425 and 426.

In the 1930s and 1940s, as the diesel came into its own, GE developed a highly successful, long-running line of 25-to-95-ton switchers for industrial, short line and branch line use. But the road diesel took a back seat at Erie, as GE focused instead on mainline electric locomotives. Between 1940 and 1953, GE's biggest involvement with road diesels was its role in the Alco-GE partnership as the supplier of traction motors, generators and electrical equipment for locomotives designed and built by Alco.

In the 1950s, GE, still without a domestic road-unit of its own, pursued the export trade with its popular "Universal" series road units. Finally, in 1953, the Alco-GE alliance dissolved (although GE continued to supply Alco with electrical equipment),

Union Pacific AC4400CW's, Norfolk Southern Dash 9-40CW's and BNSF Dash 9-44CW's take shape on the erecting floor of Building 10 at GE's Erie, Pa., facility on April 26, 1999.

setting the stage for GE's belated entry into the domestic road-diesel market. Built between 1960 and 1977, the U25 through U50 series "U-boats" that gave GE a beachhead in the domestic market are all but extinct, but thousands of their successors soldier on.

Deep within GE's Erie complex, in the 1911-built erecting hall known simply as Building 10, workers assemble the best-selling locomotives in North America. The FDL and HDL prime movers installed in Erie-built locomotives are delivered from GE's engine manufacturing facility in Grove City, Pa., while other components such as truck-frame castings come from as far away as Canada and Mexico. However, most of the major elements, assemblies and subassemblies that make up current-model GE locomotives are fabricated in the Erie works.

With the exception of several Dash 7 orders assembled in Mexico and Norfolk Southern Dash 9-40CW's 9245-9309, completed at the road's Juniata shop in Altoona, Pa., in

UP AC4400CW's 7163 and 7164 get finishing touches and predelivery tests along with sister AC44's, BNSF Dash 9-44CW's and a lone NS Dash 9-40CW in Building 26 at GE on May 5, 1999.

1998-99, GE has not followed EMD's recent practice of contracting out locomotive assembly. Indeed, save for these few anomalies, the thousands of Dash 7's, Dash 8's, Dash 9's, AC's and Genesis Series passenger units that dominate contemporary North American railroading have been crafted on the same erecting floor where generations of GE workers have been building locomotives for more than 90 years.

General Electric AC6000CW
Location of Equipment

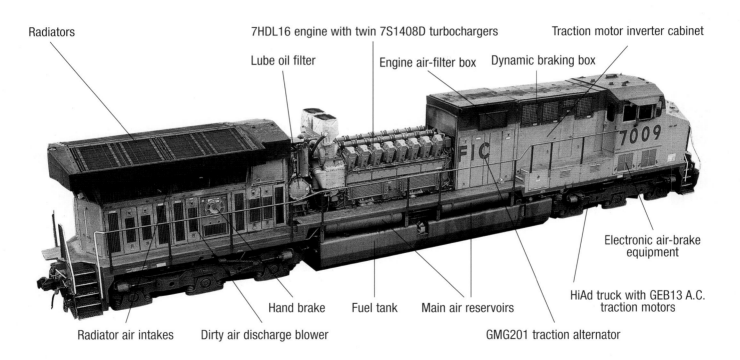

Radiators

7HDL16 engine with twin 7S1408D turbochargers

Traction motor inverter cabinet

Lube oil filter

Engine air-filter box

Dynamic braking box

Hand brake

Fuel tank

Main air reservoirs

Electronic air-brake equipment

Radiator air intakes

Dirty air discharge blower

GMG201 traction alternator

HiAd truck with GEB13 A.C. traction motors

AAR-B

FB2

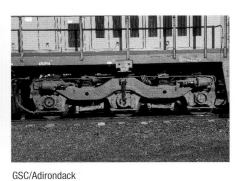

GSC/Adirondack

HiAd

Steerable

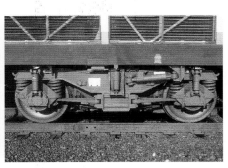

Bolsterless (passenger)

	7FDL12	7FDL16	7HDL16A
RPM Idle	450	450	440
RPM Full Load	1050	1050	1050
Stroke Cycle	4	4	4
Bore/Stroke	9 x 10 1/2"	9 x 10 1/2"	250 x 320 mm
Cylinders	12	16	16
Weight (lbs)	35,000	43,500	47,849
Aspiration	Turbocharged	Turbocharged	Turbocharged
Horsepower	3200	4400	6000

GE 7FDL16

The four-cycle, FDL Series diesel engine, a Cooper-Bessemer design, has been the standard prime mover in General Electric locomotives for more than 40 years. Rated at 2400 h.p., the 16-cylinder Cooper-Bessemer FDL powered the XP24-model U25B testbeds in 1959 and was uprated to 2500 h.p. with the introduction of production U25B's in 1960.

General Electric soon purchased the rights to the FDL engine and began producing it in its Grove City, Pa., engine plant under the GE name. Grove City continues to manufacture FDL's in 12- and 16-cylinder versions for domestic GE locomotives, but the horsepower of the venerable prime mover has nearly doubled. Through continuous refinements and upgrades, GE has managed to boost the power of the FDL16 from the 2400-h.p. rating of the XP24 to 4400 h.p. in current Dash 9 and AC locomotives.

Beyond the practical limits of the FDL, the 6000-h.p. rating of the

GE 7HDL16A

AC6000CW required GE to develop a new engine. In concert with Deutz MWM of Mannheim, Germany, GE worked to develop and perfect the 16-cylinder, 250mm-bore, 320mm-stroke 7HDL16A prime mover as the power plant for the 6000-h.p., A.C. traction AC6000CW. Like its FDL counterpart, the four-stroke, twin-turbo, 47,849-lb. HDL engine is also manufactured at Grove City.

The slight increase in hood width, evident between the "R" and "A" in Conrail, identifies CR 1954 as a Dash 7. Six power-assembly access doors ahead of the notch in the hood indicate the presence of a 12-cylinder engine, confirming that the unit is a B23-7. Buffalo, N.Y., June 9, 1988.

	B23-7	BQ23-7
Production Dates	1977-09 to 1984-05	1978-08 to 1978-09
Total Built	535	10
Length	62'2"	62'2"
Engine	7FDL12	7FDL12
Horsepower	2250	2250
Alternator	GTA11	GTA11
Traction Motors	752	752
Weight x 1000 lb	253-280	267

B23-7
U-boat styling, with Dash 7 features:
- Oversize radiators; sight increase in width of rear section of engine hood.
- Six power-assembly access doors, indicating 12-cylinder FDL engine.
- AAR-B or FB2 trucks GE standard.
- SCL 5100-5114, 5140-5154 built with trade-in EMD Blomberg trucks.
- Southern 3970-4023 built with high short hood; long-hood forward.

BQ23-7
- Enlarged Quarters Cab positioned at front of locomotive; no nose.
- Carbody similar to B23-7.
- Built on trade-in EMD Blomberg trucks.
- SCL 5130-5139 only units built.

General Electric's Dash 7 series models began replacing the legendary U-boat line in the fall of 1976 with the release of 10 C30-7's built for Burlington Northern. However, the B23-7 did not succeed the U23B until a year later. Conrail received the last U23B's in June 1977 and took delivery of the first B23-7's 3 months later, in September 1977.

The external differences between the B23-7 and U23B included an additional 2 feet in overall length, larger radiators and a stepped increase in the width of the rear section of the engine hood. The hood was widened from just ahead of the exhaust stack to the radiator cab to allow the relocation of the oil cooler—just one of many Dash 7 improvements.

More significant but less obvious Dash 7 enhancements included improvements in fuel efficiency, increased tractive effort and marked advancements in performance and reliability. GE continued to improve and refine the Dash 7 design

throughout the line's decade-long run, achieving notable increases in such critical areas as reliability and fuel efficiency, which improved by 16 percent over the production period.

The first four-axle Dash 7 model, the B23-7 was also one of the line's best-sellers. Conrail purchased not only the first, but the most, B23-7's,

assembling a fleet of 141 units in just 2 years; with a total of 123 units, Nacionales de Mexico came a close second. Nearly half of the NdeM B23-7's were assembled in the road's Aguascaliente shops from kits supplied by GE Erie, and 10 units delivered in December 1979 were built by GE in Brazil. The neighboring

Built in April 1980, Santa Fe B23-7 6401 rides FB2 trucks and features the large "silencer" exhaust stack introduced in 1979 to meet EPA noise-reduction regulations. W. Perrin, Ariz., May 1, 1996. *David R. Busse*

Ferrocariles Unidos del Sureste received a trio of Brazilian-built B23-7's at the same time.

The B23-7 was the first model to feature GE's new floating bolster FB2 truck as standard equipment. Conrail, however, opted for AAR type B trucks on its entire B23 fleet, and Santa Fe took 34 of its 69 B23's on AAR-B's. Southern's 54 B23-7's rode on stock FB2 trucks, but, in keeping with tradition, all were built with high short hoods and set up for long-hood forward operation.

Following a longstanding practice dating back to Seaboard Air Line U30B's built in 1966-67, Family Lines System's 40 Seaboard Coast Line B23-7's were delivered riding reconditioned Blomberg trucks from EMD trade-ins. However, the customization of 10 of the SCL units went far beyond the use of EMD Blomberg trucks. Designated BQ23-7's ("Q" standing for Quarters Cab), SCL 5130-5139 emerged from Erie in the fall of 1978 with flat-faced, oversized crew cabs positioned at the very front of the locomotive platform.

Outfitted with a small fuel tank to reduce axle-loading, FNM B23-7 10023 idles at Aguascalientes—the city of its birth—on November 6, 1989. Built in 1981, the lightweight GE is one of at least 64 NdeM B23-7's assembled at the road's Aguascalientes shops using kits shipped from Erie. *Robert E. Lambrecht*

The boxy cab was designed to accommodate extra crew members on the head end of cabooseless trains and included additional seating, a conductor's desk and locker space. An awkward application at best, the concept did not catch on and the 10 SCL units were the only BQ23-7's built.

Customized to a far lesser degree than the SCL BQ23-7's, Southern's 54 B23-7's were built, as illustrated by SOU 3992 at Greensboro, N.C., on January 8, 1984, with the road's customary high short hood. *Bob Graham, Mark R. Lynn collection*

Customized with Quarters Cabs designed to accommodate extra crew members on the head-end of cabooseless trains, Seaboard Coast Line 5130-5139 were the only BQ23-7's built. Following a practice dating back to Seaboard Air Line U30B's of 1966-67, SCL's 10 BQ23-7's and 30 standard B23-7's were delivered riding reconditioned Blomberg trucks from EMD trade-ins. SCL 5139 is shown at Tampa, Fla., on October 26, 1980. *Paul E. DeFries, Mark R. Lynn collection*

Delivered from Erie in December 1977, Frisco 863-870 were the first B30-7's built. The last unit of the order, SL-SF 870, heads up a string of EMD Geeps at Fort Smith, Ark., on June 29, 1979. *Michael Condren*

DASH 7 FEATURES

Oversize radiators; stepped increase in width of rear section of engine hood.

B30-7
- Carbody similar to B23-7, but eight power-assembly access doors, indicating 16-cylinder FDL engine, vs six in B23-7.
- FB2 trucks standard; some, including SL-SF 863-870, C&O 8255-8278, built with trade-in AAR-B trucks.

B30-7A
- Carbody identical to B23-7, including six power-assembly access doors, indicating 12-cylinder, 3000-h.p. FDL engine.
- FB2 trucks standard.
- MP 4667-4669, 4800-4854 only units built.

B30-7A(B)
- Cabless version of B30-7A.
- BN 4000-4119 only units built.
- BN 4053-4119 have equipment blower at forward end of unit, with dynamic brake equipment in box above air intake.
- All units built with FB2 trucks.

B30-7A1
- Carbody similar to B30-7A, but with air intakes behind cab.
- Six power-assembly access doors indicating 12-cylinder FDL engine.
- Southern 3500-3521, with high short hoods and FB2 trucks, only units built.

	B30-7	B30-7A	B30-7A(B)	B30-7A1
Production Dates	1977-12 to 1981-05	1980-06 to 1982-02	1982-06 to 1983-10	1982-04 to 1982-05
Total Built	199	58	120	22
Length	62'2"	62'2"	62'2"	62'4"
Engine	7FDL16	7FDL12	7FDL12	7FDL12
Horsepower	3000	3000	3000	3000
Alternator	GTA24	GTA24	GTA24	GTA24
Traction Motors	752	752	752	752
Weight x 1000 lb	253-280	253-280	253-280	253-280

More than 2 years after receiving the last U30B's built, Frisco was first in line for the model's successor, the B30-7. Carrying road numbers that picked up right where the U30B's left off, SL-SF B30-7's 863-870 emerged from Erie in December 1977. Looking all but identical to the B23-7, which had been introduced just 3 months earlier, the B30-7 possessed all the standard Dash 7 features, from the large radiators to the built-out rear section of the engine hood. Short of counting power-assembly access doors on the engine hood—8 for the B30's 16-cylinder engine, 6 for the B23's 12-cylinder engine—distinguishing the 3000-h.p. B30-7 from its 2000-h.p. counterpart is difficult at best.

Although the B30-7 made its debut riding the AAR-B trucks of traded-in Frisco U25B's, most roads ordered the model with floating bolster FB2 trucks. In fact, of the 199 B30-7's built, all but Frisco's 8 and 24 of C&O's 64 units—also built with AAR-B's—were outfitted with FB2 trucks.

Fresh from Erie, SP B30-7 7800 rests at Buffalo, N.Y., on its first trip, on January 4, 1978. Eight engine-hood doors, necessary to access the unit's 16-cylinder FDL prime mover, differentiate the B30-7 from the otherwise identical B23-7.

Beginning in January 1980, GE began equipping units with a noticeably fatter "silencer" exhaust stack in response to the Environmental Protection Agency's newly implemented wayside noise limits. The fat stack gave the B30-7 a distinctive look, and a muted voice, but the noise-reducing alterations were minor compared to the changes made under the hood a few months later.

In June 1980, the last three units of a Missouri Pacific B23-7 order were outshopped from Erie with their 12-cylinder engines uprated to 3000 h.p. It was a bold move, but

SP B30-7 7800

the experiment was a success, netting the railroad savings in fuel and maintenance costs and earning GE orders for a new model: the 12-cylinder, 3000-h.p. B30-7A.

MoPac purchased 55 more B30-7A's, all of which were delivered between November 1981 and

But for the road number and builder's plate, there is little to distinguish Missouri Pacific 4809 and its B30-7A kin from the B23-7. Powered by 12-cylinder FDL engines, the two models are externally identical.

February 1982. Not surprisingly, road numbers and builder's plates were the only reliable way to differentiate MP B30-7A's 4800-4854 from their B23-7 kin.

Following MoPac's lead, Southern ordered 22 12-cylinder B30's configured, as usual, with high short hoods and long-hood forward. The Southern units were built with a slightly different machinery layout, having the equipment blower relocated from the radiator end of the locomotive to a position between the prime mover and the cab. Although the differences are slight, GE classed Southern 3500-3521—the only ones built—as B30-7A1.

Burlington Northern bought into the 3000-h.p., 12-cylinder concept with even greater enthusiasm. However, there would be no mistaking BN's B30-7A's for anything else, as all 120 were built as cabless B-units. GE made no change in the model designation to indicate the absence of a cab, but the informal convention has been to refer to the cabless units as B30-7A(B). The BN units were built in two orders; the first 53 were delivered from June to August 1982, with the remaining 67 following from August to October 1983. In an arrangement similar to the B30-7A1, the second order had the equipment blower relocated to the forward section of the locomotive, just ahead of the prime mover. This configuration displaced the dynamic brake equipment, which was moved upward and contained in a large box projecting above the hood-line.

Furnished with high short hoods in the Southern tradition, SOU B30-7A1's 3500-3521 were the only examples of the model built. As indicated by the air intakes next to the cab of SOU 3515, the difference between the B30-7A1 and the standard B30-7 is the relocation of the equipment blower from the radiator compartment to the cab end of the hood. This modification was necessary to accommodate more powerful dynamic brakes as specified by the railroad.

Differences between the first and second orders of cabless Burlington Northern B30-7A's are evidenced by "Phase I" BN 4020 near Ash Hill, Calif., on November 26, 1997, and "Phase II" Central Michigan 2001 (ex-BN 4054), at Bay City, Mich., August 3, 2000. An almost featureless hood identifies the first order, BN 4000-4052, built in 1982, while the relocation of dynamic brake equipment to a large box projecting above the hood-line readily identifies the second group built in 1983 as BN 4053-4119. BNSF retired its entire fleet of cabless B30-7A's in 1999, but a few have found new homes, including three on Central Michigan and five on Providence & Worcester.

The second-last B30-7 built, CSXT 5579 lifts out of Wartrace, Tenn., leading D&H GP39-2 7418 and B30-7 5528 on southbound train R675 on April 15, 1991. Still wearing its original Chessie System paint and riding the AAR-B trucks of a U25B trade-in, the 5579 was built as C&O 8297 and is outfitted with the large "silencer" exhaust stack found on most units built after 1979.

A short-lived feature of early B36-7's, baffle plates shielding the radiator section equip Sante Fe 7491. Designed to reduce noise from the radiator fan, the plates were installed on the first three B36-7 orders, but were ultimately removed. *David R. Busse*

	B36-7
Production Dates	1980-01 to 1985-09
Total Built	230
Length	62'2"
Engine	7FDL16
Horsepower	3000
Alternator	GTA24
Traction Motors	752AF
Weight x 1000 lb	259–280

DASH 7 FEATURES
- Oversize radiators; stepped increase in width of rear section of engine hood.

B36-7
- Identical to B30-7; eight power-assembly access doors indicating 16-cylinder FDL engine.
- FB2 trucks standard.
- Large "silencer" exhaust stack standard.
- Blank headlight box in nose eliminated after first order.
- Southern 3815-3820 built with high short hood; long-hood forward.

The he B36-7 evolved directly from and is externally identical to the B30-7. In fact, the first B36-7 testbeds were four B30-7's upgraded to 3600 h.p. on the factory floor at Erie. The first units of a Cotton Belt order for 30 B30-7's, SSW 7770-7773 were outshopped in January 1980 with GE's new Sentry adhesion-control system, high-capacity GTA24 alternators, upgraded 752AF traction motors and 16-cylinder FDL engines rated at 3600 h.p. Subjected to exhaustive predelivery tests and rigorous road trials on SP, the quartet of 3600-h.p. prototypes performed satisfactorily, and the B36-7 was born.

The first production B36-7's, Santa Fe 7484-7499, were delivered in the fall of 1980, followed by a half-dozen high-nose versions built for Southern in the spring of 1981. In 1983-84, Exxon exported eight B36-7's to one of its South American operations in Colombia, but on the home front, sales of the 3600-h.p. Dash 7 were lagging. Conrail gave

Less than a year old, Conrail B36-7's 5023, 5027 and 5021 lead GP40-2 3270 on TV9 at Lackawanna, N.Y., June 21, 1984.

the model a boost with the acquisition of 60 units in late 1983, while Southern Pacific added 16 B36-7's to its stable in November and December 1984.

After 4 years, total B36-7 production stood at a mere 110 units, but with the stroke of a pen, Seaboard System more than doubled the figure, ordering 120 units for delivery in two 1985 orders. Completed at Erie between February and September 1985, SBD 5806-5925 were the last B36-7's built.

In keeping with the road's long-standing tradition, Southern's six B36-7's were constructed with high short hoods and set up for long-hood forward operation. Built in March 1981, Southern 3815-3820 were the road's last high-nose GE's. Wearing NS paint, 3815 keeps company with high-nose GP50 7043 at Ludlow, Ky., on September 21, 1988.

Seaboard System B36-7 5882 and five sisters line up at the Belt Railway of Chicago's Clearing Yard in Bedford Park, Ill., on January 26, 1987. SBD more than doubled total production of the 3600 h.p. B-B model with the purchase of 120 units. Delivered in 1985, SBD 5806-5925 were the last B36-7's built.

The only B32-8's built were BN-painted testbeds 5497-5499, outshopped in January 1984. Last of the three, BN 5499 poses at Lincoln, Nebr., on March 30, 1985. *Robert E. Lambrecht*

	B32-8	B36-8	B39-8
Production Dates	1984-01	1982-10	1984-01 to 1988-04
Total Built	3	1	145
Length	63'7"	66'4"	66'4"
Engine	7FDL12	7FDL16	7FDL16
Horsepower	3150	3600	3900
Alternator	GMG186	GMG186A1	GMG186A1
Traction Motors	752AG	752AG	752AG
Weight x 1000 lb	262-280	274-280	274-280

B32-8
- Boxy, beveled nose, sharp-angled features, including oversize radiators.
- Roof-line of curved-top cab lower than dynamic brake and equipment blower box.
- Step in hood, similar to Dash 7; six power-assembly access doors, indicating 12-cylinder FDL engine.
- FB2 trucks standard.
- BN 5497-5499 only units built.

B36-8
- Carbody similar to B32-8, but unit nearly 3 feet longer.
- Eight power-assembly access doors indicating 16-cylinder FDL engine.
- GE 606 only unit built; upgraded to B39-8.

B39-8 (Testbed version)
- Carbody similar to B32-8, but unit nearly 3 feet longer.
- Eight power-assembly access doors indicating 16-cylinder FDL engine.
- ATSF 7400-7402 only units built.

B39-8 (Production version)
- Flat-top cab, roof-line flush with equipment blower and dynamic brake box.
- Angled air-intakes below oversize radiators. No step in engine hood.
- Eight power-assembly access doors indicating 16-cylinder FDL engine.
- FB2 trucks standard.

Generals Electric's Dash 8 locomotive series was the product of a development program launched in 1980 to improve upon Dash 7 technology and performance, particularly in the areas of fuel efficiency and tractive effort. The first Dash 8, a 3600-horsepower, B-B, B36-8 prototype numbered 606, was outshopped from Erie in October 1982.

The starkly styled appearance of the 606, with its boxy nose, sharp-angled features, oversize radiators and FB2 trucks, heralded not only a new look, but a new generation of General Electric diesels. With microprocessor control systems and a computerized Microsentry Adhesion System, a newly designed GMG alternator and improved 752AG traction motors, the Dash 8 would not only lead GE into dieseldom's third generation, but solidify the company's recently established position as North America's number-one locomotive builder.

Strictly a prototype, GE 606 stuck close to Erie as engineers continued

The original Dash 8, and one of the most heavily modified locomotives in GE's test fleet, B39-8 809 (built as B36-8 606) stands outside the test house at Erie on April 14, 1989, having recently been outfitted with its third cab, the prototype version of GE's North American cab.

development of the Dash 8 design. In March 1983, the 606 was joined by a six-axle C36-8 testbed numbered 607. The pair underwent exhaustive tests and numerous modifications as the Dash 8 concept was refined. A true guinea pig, the pioneer Dash 8 has undergone uncounted rebuilds and is one of the most heavily modified locomotives in GE's test fleet. In 1986, the unit was rebuilt with enhanced Dash 8 features,

The curved-top cab, its roof-line lower than that of the dynamic brake and blower boxes behind it, along with vertical, rather than angled, air intakes beneath the radiators, gives early Dash 8's an unmistakable look. Only seven B-B Dash 8's were built in this configuration: GE B36-7 606, BN B32-8 testbeds 5497-5499 and Santa Fe B39-8 testbeds 7400-7402. Santa Fe's first Dash 8, B39-8 7400, rests at Corwith Yard in Chicago, Ill., in the company of GP50 3848 on July 12, 1986.

A half-dozen four-axle prototypes were outshopped in 1984, including three 3150-h.p. B32-8's delivered as Burlington Northern 5497-5499 and three 3900-h.p. B39-8's built as Santa Fe 7400-7402.

Similar in appearance to GE 606, the testbeds are readily distinguishable from later Dash 8's by a number of features that were not carried over into regular Dash 8 production. A legacy of the Dash 7, the testbeds were built with "stepped" engine hoods that widened just ahead of the exhaust stack. However, the most noticeable feature is the squat, curved-roof cab that sits slightly lower than the equipment blower and dynamic brake boxes immediately behind it. Production Dash 8's (with the exception of early C39-8's) feature a flat-top cab extended to the same height and flush with the equipment boxes.

Based on test data and experience with the BN and Santa Fe testbeds, as well as prototype 606, GE enhanced the Dash 8 design. The production version of the

upgraded to 3900 h.p. and renumbered 808. In 1988, the locomotive was outfitted with a prototype design for GE's version of the Canadian comfort cab and renumbered 809. Still sporting the one-of-a-kind cab, 809 remains an active member of the GE test fleet stabled at Erie.

In lieu of fielding Dash 8 demonstrators, GE constructed a small fleet of 18 preproduction, builder-owned testbeds, which were supplied to several railroads for long-term evaluation in revenue service.

The production version of the B39-8 incorporated a host of refinements, the most noticeable of which is a flat-top cab, extended to a height flush with the equipment boxes. More subtle changes include angled air-intakes below the radiators and the disappearance of the Dash 7-style "step" in the engine hood. One of the first production Dash 8's, LMX B39-8 8502—still unlettered—works out on the GE test track east of Erie, Pa., on July 1, 1987.

Only two production orders of B39-8's, LMX 8500-8599 and Southern Pacific 8000-8039, were built before the model was upgraded to the Dash 8-40B. In near sequential order, SP 8032-8033-8035 and 8034 depart Colton, Calif., on December 26, 1987. *David R. Busse*

B39-8 incorporated a host of refinements, including a single-fan radiator cooling system (versus two fans in the testbeds), modified air intakes, an air-cooled, A.C.-motor-driven compressor, simplified wiring and a redesigned dynamic brake and an enlarged cab.

GE began outshopping the first production-model B39-8's in 1987, 100 LMX units for long-term "power-by-the-hour" lease to Burlington Northern and 40 units for Southern Pacific. Even as the new B39's rolled out of Erie, GE continued to refine and improve the Dash 8 design. By 1988, GE deemed the design

advances to be significant enough to warrant a nominal increase in horsepower rating and a new model designation. In April 1988, as the last LMX B39-8's neared completion, they shared the shop floor at Erie with the first examples of their successor model, the Dash 8-40B.

Running long-hood forward, Norfolk Southern 3549 leads a westbound RoadRailer out of Buffalo, N.Y., on August 16, 1990. NS purchased the only Dash 8-32B's, but GE built a single unit, numbered 832, for its own use.

Constructed with low noses, Norfolk Southern Dash 8-32B's 3522-3566 have the long-hood end designated as the front of the locomotive, but operate in either direction, as evidenced by brand-new 3546 at Fort Erie, Ont., on December 5, 1989.

	DASH 8-32B	DASH 8-32BWH
Production Dates	1989-09 to 1989-12	1991-08 to 1991-12
Total Built	46	20
Length	63'7"	66'4"
Engine	7FDL12	7FDL12
Horsepower	3200	3200
Alternator	GMG186	GMG186
Traction Motors	752AG	752AG
Weight x 1000 lb	284	264.5

DASH 8-32B
- Nearly 3 feet shorter than, but similar carbody to, production B39-8/Dash 8-40B.
- Six power-assembly access doors indicating 12-cylinder FDL engine, vs eight for B39-8/Dash 8-40B.
- NS 3522-3566, GE 832 only units built.

DASH 8-32BWH
- North American cab.
- Carbody similar to Dash 8-40BW, but six power-assembly access doors indicating 12-cylinder FDL engine, vs eight for Dash 8-40BW.
- Amtrak 500-519 only units built.

The B32-8 and its Dash 8-32B successor were largely overlooked as railroads followed the trend toward high-horsepower B-B's in the mid to late 1980s. Although the BN B32-8's were among the first Dash 8's on the road, the model received no orders. Nevertheless, GE retained the medium-horsepower model in its revamped Dash 8 line, offering both the four-axle Dash 8-32B and a six-axle Dash 8-32C in its 1988 catalog. No buyers were found for the Dash 8-32C, but in 1989, Norfolk Southern ordered 45 Dash 8-32B's. Turned out between September and December '89, Norfolk Southern 3522-3566 and GE 832—built to NS specs and assigned to the Erie test facility— are the only Dash 8-32B's built.

Just under 3 feet shorter than the Dash 8-40B, the 12-cylinder, 3200-h.p. Dash 8-32B is similar in appearance to its 16-cylinder, 4000-h.p. big brother. The shorter overall length of the locomotive, along with a smaller engine hood sporting six instead of eight access doors, both indicative of the 12-cylinder engine, distinguish the Dash 8-32B from its more numerous '40B kin.

Amtrak took a variation on the B32 concept in 1991, commissioning GE to build 20 customized Dash 8-32BWH passenger engines as part of a 52-unit order that included the first Genesis locomotives. Basically the Dash 8-32BWH—or P32BH, as Amtrak designates it—is a Dash 8-32B with a North American cab and head-end power. To accommodate the second alternator required for HEP generation, the locomotives are constructed on the slightly longer Dash 8-40BW platform. Other modifications made to adapt the locomotive for passenger service include the addition of a fourth microprocessor control system and dozens of engineering and design changes made to meet Amtrak weight restrictions.

Amtrak Dash 8-32BWH 500, the first of only 20 built, leads F40PH 238 out of Salinas, Calif., with No. 11, the *Coast Starlight*, on November 8, 1993.

The Dash 8-40B, introduced in April 1988, is outwardly identical to its B39-8 predecessor, as shown by Susquehanna Dash 8-40B 4006 at Buffalo, N.Y., on March 8, 1989.

	DASH 8-40B	DASH 8-40BW
Production Dates	1988-04 to 1989-05	1991-08 to 1991-12
Total Built	151	83
Length	66′4″	66′4″
Engine	7FDL16	7FDL16
Horsepower	4000	4000
Alternator	GMG186	GMG186
Traction Motors	752AG	752AG
Weight x 1000 lb	288	289

DASH 8-40B
- Almost identical to production version of B39-8.
- Flat-top cab, flush with equipment blower and dynamic brake box.
- Angled air-intakes below oversize radiators.
- Eight power-assembly access doors indicating 16-cylinder FDL engine.
- FB2 trucks standard.

DASH 8-40BW
- North American cab; rest of carbody similar to Dash 8-40B.
- Dynamic brake vents relocated to right side of hood, immediately behind cab.
- ATSF 500-582 only units built.

Coincident with numerous design changes and improvements to the Dash 8 line in 1988, GE revised its model-designation formula and reversed the conventional nomenclature. Thus, the new 4000-h.p., B-B hood, which would have previously been labeled simply B40-8, was introduced as the Dash 8-40B. Some railroads found the new terminology cumbersome and stuck with the simpler model designation for their own purposes. Whatever the label, the Dash 8-40B proved to be the apex of the four-motor Dash 8 line.

Outwardly indistinguishable from the production model B39-8, the Dash 8-40B incorporated a host of internal enhancements, from software upgrades and redesigned components to improved performance of the 7FDL16 engine. Born to run, the Dash 8-40B found its niche in high-speed intermodal service. In 1988-89, Conrail, Cotton Belt, Santa Fe and even Susquehanna purchased B40's to power their hottest trains. Two single-unit orders, one for the

Purchased in 1988 for intermodal service, Conrail 5060-5089 were the first Dash 8-40B's. Performing in their intended role, 5063, 5068 and 5079 lead TV10 at Tifft St. in Buffalo, N.Y., on May 18, 1989.

Department of Energy's Savannah River Project, the other a GECX lease unit, rounded out Dash 8-40B production to 151 units in just over one year. However, the ever-increasing length and tonnage of double-stack and piggyback trains prompted roads to shift to six-axle power for intermodal trains, and B40 sales dried up.

Santa Fe, a Dash 8 devotee since the days of the B39-8 testbeds, stuck with the B40 long enough to give the model its finest hour. In 1990, Uncle John bolstered its B40 stable with a requisition for 60 more 4000-h.p. B-B Dash 8's, all of which were to be outfitted with North American cabs and dressed in Santa Fe's newly revived Warbonnet paint. Designated Dash 8-40BW and numbered Santa Fe 500-559, the units were delivered in October and November 1990. Shortly thereafter, the road placed a followup order for 23 additional Dash 8-40BW's. Outshopped from Erie in the spring of 1992, Santa Fe 560-582 were the last four-motor Dash 8's built for road-freight service. Thus far, they also hold a place in history as the last four-motor GE's built for road-freight duty.

Santa Fe's second order of standard-cab Dash 8-40B's, Nos. 7430-7449, have their nose-mounted headlights encased by a protective frame, as illustrated by AT&SF 7442 at Erie, Pa., April 14, 1989.

The cabs of units in Santa Fe's second Dash 8-40BW order, Nos. 560-582, are fabricated with the "gull wing" profile specified for the road's six-axle Dash 8's and Dash 9's. This modification, as illustrated by 572 at Saginaw, Texas, on July 6, 1993, was made to meet clearance restrictions at the coal-loading facility at York Canyon, N. Mex. *Mark R. Lynn*

To date, the only four-motor GE freight locomotives with North American cabs are Santa Fe Dash 8-40BW's 500-582, all delivered in Warbonnet paint. Still looking like new, 548 leads the 199 train up Edelstein Hill, east of Chillicothe, Ill., on September 28, 1991.

With a Dash 8-style cab, square-edged engine hood, a U23B frame and trade-in EMD Blomberg trucks, Monongahela Super 7-B23 2305, seen at Brownsville, Pa., on November 3, 1992, is unlikely to be mistaken for anything else. Monongahela purchased 11 of the 16 Super 7-B23's built.

	SUPER 7-B23	SUPER 7-C30	SUPER 7N-C30	CMP30-S7N
Production Dates	1989-03 to 1991-02	1989-05 to 1993	1990-91	1994-08 to 1994-09
Total Built	16	111+	100	34
Length	60'2"	67'3"	67'3"	67'3"
Engine	7FDL12	7FDL16	7FDL16	7FDL16
Horsepower	2250	3000	3000	3000
Alternator	GTA24	GTA24	GTA24	GTA24
Traction Motors	752	752	752AF	752
Weight x 1000 lb	268	395	360	395

SUPER 7-B23
- Dash 8 cab, carbody, cooling system and dynamic brake on U23B platform.
- Engine hood has squared, not rounded, edges.
- All but Roberval Saguenay 50-52 built on trade-in EMD Blomberg trucks.

SUPER 7-C30
- Dash 8 cab, carbody, cooling system and dynamic brake on U30C, U33C or U36C platform and trucks.
- Engine hood has squared, not rounded, edges.

SUPER 7N-C30
- Dash 8 cab, carbody, cooling system and dynamic brake on C30-7 platform.
- All new components.
- Engine hood has squared, not rounded, edges.
- FNM only customer.

CMP30-S7N
- Dash 8 cab, carbody, cooling system and dynamic brake on C30-7 platform.
- All new components, includes microprocessor controls.
- Engine hood has squared, not rounded, edges.
- FNM 15000-15033 only units built.

In an effort to tap the short-line, regional and rebuild business, GE embarked on an aggressive campaign to develop and market a conservatively rated, reliable, but low-cost locomotive available in four- and six-axle versions. The result, unveiled in the spring of 1989, was the Super 7.

A hybrid of sorts, the Super 7 was more than just a rebuild, but not quite a new locomotive. An all-new Dash 8 cab, carbody, cooling system and dynamic braking gave the Super 7 the look, fit and feel of a new unit. However, the Super 7 platform and many of its major components, including the fuel tank, truck and traction-motor frames, engine main frame, alternator, draft gear and air-brake equipment, were reclaimed from retired GE U-series locomotives.

A unique blend of remanufactured components and new Dash 7 and Dash 8 technology, the Super 7 was new, or like-new, from the rails up. Although the locomotive's prime mover used a reclaimed main frame, the entire engine was completely

Details and differences between the left and right sides of the Super 7-B23 are evident as Conrail 2037 and 2033, formerly Monongahela 2307 and 2303, work back to back at Mingo, Jct., Ohio, on August 30, 1995.

remanufactured with Dash 8 power assemblies, injectors and turbocharger. All other recycled components were likewise remanufactured and often upgraded.

All wiring, circuitry and electronics were new, and up to late Dash 7 standards or higher. In the name of simplicity and economics, the Super 7 was not afforded the luxury of Dash 8-style microprocessors, but was equipped with an on-board computer package, including microprocessor-managed thermal

protection and Sentry adhesion control.

In the spring of 1989, GE fielded a half-dozen Super 7 demonstrators; three four-axle Super 7-B23's and three six-axle Super 7-C30's. The first unit, Super 7-B23 GECX 2000, was constructed on the platform of ex-Western Pacific U23B 2263 and emerged from Erie in March. The next two Super 7-B23's, also built from WP U23B's, and all three Super 7-C30's (built from ex-Southern U33C's 3811-3812 and UP U30C 2956)

In common with its four-axle counterpart, the Super 7-C30 features a Dash 8-style cab and a square-edged engine hood and utilizes the frame and trucks of retired U-boats. GECX 3005, on the UP at Yermo, Calif., on February 1, 1996, was built by GE in the former Montreal Locomotive Works in Montreal, Que., using the platform of retired Milwaukee Road U30C 5652.

Monongahela and 3 for Roberval & Saguenay, while the hulks of retired D&H, Milwaukee Road and Penn Central U30, U33 and U36C's were used in the construction of 11 Super 7-C30's, 8 GECX lease fleet units and 3 units for Ferrocariles Nacionales de Mexico.

The Super 7 series failed to attract serious interest from U.S. and Canadian roads, but the concept caught on in Mexico. In 1990, FNM ordered 100 all-new, Erie-built Super 7N-C30's and initiated a program to construct Super 7-C30 rebuilds in its own shops. By 1993, FNM's Aguascalientes, Concarril, Empalme and San Luis Potosi shops had constructed nearly 100 Super 7-C30's from NdeM and FCP U30C's, U36C's, U36CG's and C30-7's.

In 1994, the Super 7 joined the ranks of third-generation diesels as FNM took delivery of 34 micro-processor-equipped Super 7's. Designated CMP30-S7N, FNM 15000-15033, the ultimate in Super 7's, emerged from Erie in August and September 1994.

were built by Morrison-Knudsen's Boise, Idaho, shop under contract to GE.

With production at Erie running near capacity, General Electric assigned further Super 7 production to its recently acquired Canadian facility, the former Bombardier/ Montreal Locomotive Works plant in Montreal, Que. Employed primarily for construction of export locomotives during its short existence as a GE shop, the Montreal plant built a total of 24 Super 7's between 1989 and 1991. Former Western Pacific U23B's were used to build 10 Super 7 B23's for

Ferrocariles Nacionales de Mexico rebuilt six-axle U-boats and C30-7's to Super 7-C30's, and also received 100 all-new Super 7N-C30's and 34 built-new, microprocessor-equipped Super 7's designated CMP30-S7N. All are similar in appearance. Super 7-C30 14023, at Empalme, Sonora, on February 18, 1993, was built at FNM's Concarril shop in 1990 using the platform of a retired NdeM U36C, while FNM Super 7N-C30 14582, at Cleburne, Texas, was built new at Erie in 1991.

Left: *Mark R. Lynn*

For the most part, the C30-7 retained the classic lines of its U-boat predecessors. The slight increase in the width of the engine hood, visible just after the word "System," confirms the Dash 7 pedigree of L&N C30-7 7050, at Corbin, Ky., on April 1, 1980.

	C30-7	C30-7A
Production Dates	1976-09 to 1986-05	1984-05 to 1984-06
Total Built	1078	50
Length	67'3"	67'3"
Engine	7FDL16	7FDL12
Horsepower	3000	3000
Alternator	GTA-11	GTA-11
Traction Motors	752	752
Weight x 1000 lb	359-420	359-420

C30-7

- U-boat styling, with Dash features: Oversize radiators; stepped increase in width of rear section of engine hood.
- Eight power-assembly access doors, indicating 16-cylinder FDL engine.

C30-7A

- Similar to C30-7, but with six power-assembly access doors indicating 12-cylinder FDL engine, vs eight for C30-7.
- Conrail 6550-6599 only units built.

General Electric's Dash 7 Series, successor to the U-boat line, made its debut in September 1976 as Erie outshopped Burlington Northern C30-7 5500. The 3000-h.p. C30-7 was designed to supersede the U30C, the best-selling model in GE's legendary U-boat stable. Born in the midst of the coal boom, the C30-7 hit the ground running and not only met but nearly doubled the U30C's 600-unit domestic sales record.

Like most Dash 7's, the C30 retained the classic U-boat styling, but boasted internal improvements, including an upgraded electrical system, increased fuel efficiency and tractive effort, along with significant gains in performance and reliability. Enhancement of the Dash 7 design continued throughout the line's decade-long run. Particular emphasis was placed on improving reliability and fuel efficiency, and notable increases were achieved in both areas. Fuel economy alone was improved by 16 percent

Toiling in the service for which they were built, BN C30-7's 5549 and 5013 lead SP SD45 rebuild 8651 and BN SD40-2 7252 with eastbound coal near Crawford, Nebr., on September 17, 1997. BN's C30-7 fleet, 242 units strong, was the largest in the United States. *George McDonnell*

over the Dash 7's decade-long production period.

Larger radiators, similar to the "winged" rads of the U33C and U36C, distinguish the C30-7 from its U30C forerunner. However, the stepped engine hood, which widens just ahead of the exhaust stack in order to accommodate the relocation of the oil cooler, eliminates any

doubt that the unit is indeed a Dash 7.

Mexico embraced the C30-7 with great enthusiasm. Alco advocate Ferrocariles del Pacifico purchased 26 units, but the lion's share of the Mexican C30 fleet went NdeM, with 328 C30-7's. At least 71 of the NdeM C30-7's were assembled at the road's Aguascalientes shops, using kits shipped from Erie. An additional

Santa Fe amassed the second-largest domestic fleet of C30-7's with the purchase of 157 units between December 1977 and December 1982. Less than 4 months old, C30-7 8011, the second unit of the road's initial 10-unit order, rolls through Caliente, Calif., on March 19, 1978.

NdeM C30-7 order was canceled after GE had begun production. Ironically, after languishing in the back lot at Erie for years, many of the platforms built for the terminated order eventually made it to Mexico—employed in the construction of NdeM Super 7N-C30's in 1990-91.

Four years after introducing the 12-cylinder, 3000-h.p. B30-7A, GE applied the concept to a six-motor model. While the B30-7A sold a respectable 200 units—including 120 cabless units to BN—the 12-cylinder, 3000-h.p. C30-7A found only one taker. Delivered in the spring of 1984, Conrail 6550-6599 were the only C30-7A's built.

Otherwise similar to the standard C30-7, the 50 C30-7A's can be identified by the presence of six engine-hood access doors rather than the normal eight doors found on the 16-cylinder model.

Conrail 6550-6599 were the only C30-7A's built. Sub-lettered "NS" for its new owner, CR 6593 switches at Buffalo, N.Y., on June 22, 1999. But for the 12-cylinder FDL beneath its hood, as indicated by six, rather than eight, power-assembly access doors, the C30-7A is little different from its 16-cylinder C30-7 counterpart.

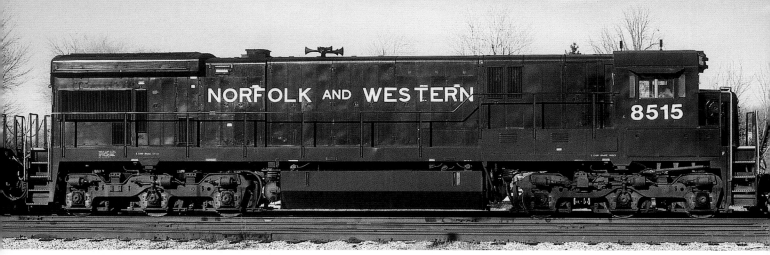

Early C36-7's, such as N&W 8515 at St. Thomas, Ont., on November 27, 1986, are outwardly identical to C30-7's.

	C36-7
Production Dates	1978-06 to 1985-11
Total Built	169
Length	67'3"
Engine	7FDL16
Horsepower	3600 (84 units) 3750 (85 units)
Alternator	GTA-24
Traction Motors	725AF
Weight x 1000 lb	366-420

C36-7
• Early versions similar to C30-7.
• Some Dash 8-style features incorporated in later orders.
• NS 8531-8542, MP 9000-9059 built with Dash 8-style equipment blower and dynamic brakes.
• CR 6620-6644, MP 9000-9059 rated at 3750 h.p.

Ever pushing the horsepower envelope, Erie outshopped GE 505, an Engineering Department test unit and 3600-h.p. C36-7 prototype, in June 1978. Outwardly identical to the C30, the first production C36-7's were built for Mexico, with 10 constructed for NdeM in March 1979 and 15 for FCP several months later. In 1980, NdeM boosted its C36-7 fleet to 25 with the receipt of 15 Brazilian-built units delivered from GE of Brazil between March and May.

The C36-7 did not break into the domestic market until the March 1981 delivery of Norfolk & Western 8500-8505. N&W remained the sole C36-7 customer for several years, purchasing a total of 43 units by May 1984.

Sluggish sales did not stop GE from working to enhance the C36-7 design—even after Dash 8 models had entered production. In May 1984, N&W 8531-8542 were delivered with Dash 8-style equipment blower and dynamic brake boxes. A month later, Conrail—a new C36-7 customer —took delivery of 25 units. Conrail

As the C36-7 evolved, several Dash 8-style features were incorporated into the design. Modified with enlarged air-intakes and Dash 8-style dynamic brakes in a large box behind the cab, GE C36-7 testbed 505 works the test track east of Erie with CN Dash 8-40CM's on March 1, 1990. The 505 was scrapped in 1995.

6620-6644 retained the old C30 carbody but were rated at 3750 h.p.

Dash 8 production was in full swing when GE filled the final domestic C36-7 order, 60 units for Missouri Pacific. Outshopped between September and November 1985 wearing UP armor yellow with Missouri Pacific lettering, MP 9000-9059 were rated at 3750 h.p. and equipped with a number of Dash 8-type features, including the

Norfolk & Western's third and final C36-7 order, Nos. 8531-8542 were built in May 1984 with the enlarged equipment blower and Dash 8-style dynamic brake equipment tested on GE 505. Operating long-hood forward, C36-7 8535 leads C39-8 8588 at Buffalo, N.Y., on June 9, 1988.

enlarged equipment blower and dynamic brake boxes employed on N&W 8531-8542.

Although the MP order marked the end of domestic production of the model, Erie had not built its last C36-7's. Between July 1984 and April 1986, Erie turned out 420 C36-7's for China's Ministry of Railways. The Chinese contract, split in two orders, is notable not just for its size but for the fact that it kept the Erie plant in business through one of the leanest periods in recent times.

A final C36-7 footnote is the import of three secondhand Australian-built units in the year 2000. Built by Australian licensee Goninan in May 1978, retired Hamersley Iron C36-7's 5057-5059 were purchased by National Railway Equipment and brought to the United States, along with several ex-Hamersley Australian-built SD50's. Hamersley 5059 was sold to Minnesota Commercial, while 5057-5058 joined NRE's lease fleet.

Posed at Dolton, Ill., in September 1987, MP C36-7's 9038, 9057 and 9048 (detail view), illustrate the final version of the C36-7. Rated at 3750 h.p. and equipped with a number of Dash 8-type features, MP 9000-9059 were built between September and November 1985 and delivered in Union Pacific paint with Missouri Pacific lettering.

The first six-axle Dash 8, GE 607 was built in March 1983 as a C36-8 and has been continuously modified and upgraded. Renumbered GE 609, the unit tested briefly as a coal-fired diesel testbed in the late 1980s. In 1999, the pioneer Dash 8 was stripped to the frame and rebuilt to Dash 9 specifications to serve in emissions testing programs as GE 899.

C32-8

- Boxy, beveled nose; sharp-angled features, including oversize radiators.
- Roof-line of curved-top cab lower than dynamic brake and equipment blower box.
- Step in hood, similar to Dash 7; six power-assembly access doors, indicating 12-cylinder FDL engine.
- Nearly 3 feet shorter than C39-8.
- CR 6610-6619 (GE prototype testbeds) only units built.

C36-8

- Identical to early C39-8.
- GE 607 only unit built.
- Upgraded to C39-8.

C39-8

- Carbody similar to C32-8, but unit nearly 3 feet longer.
- Eight power-assembly access doors, indicating 16-cylinder FDL engine, vs six for C32-8.

C39-8 (final version)

- Flat-top cab, roof-line flush with equipment blower and dynamic brake box.
- Angled air-intakes below oversize radiators. No step in engine hood.
- Cross-mounted air reservoirs at front and rear of fuel tank.
- NS 8664-8688 only units built.

	C32-8	C36-8	C39-8
Production Dates	1984-09	1983-03	1984-01 to 1987-06
Total Built	10	1	161
Length	67'11"	70'8"	70'8"
Engine	7FDL12	7FDL16	7FDL16
Horsepower	3150	3600	3900
Alternator	GMG187	GMG187	GMG187
Traction Motors	752	752	752
Weight x 1000 lb	346-420	365-420	365-420

Following the October 1982 completion of prototype B36-8 606, the second phase of GE's Dash 8 development program included the construction of a 3600-h.p., six-motor testbed. The first C-C Dash 8, GE C36-8 607 was outshopped in March 1983. Looking like an elongated version of the 606, GE 607 featured the same stark styling and sharp-angled features, with oversize radiators, a boxy nose and a conventional curved-roof cab that sat lower than the equipment blower and dynamic brake boxes immediately behind it.

The odd-looking pair were subjected to exhaustive testing and extensive modifications as GE engineers worked to refine the Dash 8 concept. Upgraded to 3900 horsepower, the original six-axle Dash 8 was joined by a pair of preproduction C39-8's outshopped for Norfolk Southern in January 1984. Part of the 18-unit fleet of builder-owned, preproduction Dash 8's supplied to several railroads for long-term evaluation, NS 8550-8551 were similar in

The "camelback" look of early Dash 8's, with the dynamic brake and blower box sitting higher than the roof-line of the curved-top cab, is apparent as Norfolk Southern C39-8's 8633 and 8634 idle at Buffalo, N.Y., on July 22, 1986. Unlike its four-axle counterpart, the production version of the C39-8 is externally identical to the preproduction testbeds.

appearance to GE 607, but dressed in full Norfolk Southern paint.

In September 1984, the final group of preproduction testbeds, 10 Conrail C32-8's, were released from Erie. Powered by 12-cylinder FDL engines rated at 3150 h.p., CR 6610-6619 were in effect a Dash 8 version of the C30-7A. Externally, the units appeared similar to GE 607 and NS 8550-8551, with the exception of the six-door engine-hood configura-

tion indicative of their 12-cylinder engine. Like the C30-7A, the C32-8 found no takers other than Conrail, and the 10 testbeds were the only examples of the model built.

The C39-8 was first Dash 8 model to enter full production. More or less identical to testbeds 8550-8551, Norfolk Southern C39-8's 8552-8563 began rolling off the assembly line at Erie in October 1984—only months after the preproduction duo hit the road. Within two years, NS would take delivery of 100 more C39-8's in the so-called "classic" configuration with the low-profile, rounded-roof cab. Conrail, the only other road to purchase C39-8's, took delivery of 22 similar units in the summer of 1986.

Major design enhancements and improvements in the Dash 8 design, including software upgrades, the introduction of a single-fan radiator cooling system (versus two fans in earlier production), modified air intakes, an air-cooled A.C.-motor-driven air compressor, simplified wiring, a redesigned dynamic brake and an enlarged cab, were incorporated into the final C39-8 order. Built between March and June 1987, NS C39-8's 8664-8688 forecast the configuration, componentry and look of the model that would succeed them: the Dash 8-40C.

Delivered in the summer of 1986, Conrail 6000-6021 were the only C39-8's sold to a railroad other than Norfolk Southern. Last of the order, CR 6021 stands in the company of BNSF Dash 9-44CW 968 at Clyde Yard in Cicero, Ill., on September 21, 1997.

In 1984, Conrail took delivery of preproduction C32-8's 6610-6619. Powered by a 12-cylinder FDL engine, the 3150-h.p. testbeds were nearly 3 feet shorter than the 3900-h.p., 16-cylinder C39-8, but similar in overall appearance. Other than the difference in length, the six-door engine hood—corresponding with the 12-cylinder prime mover—is the only major external distinction between the C32-8 and the C39-8. The 10 Conrail testbeds were the only C32-8's built.

The last C39-8's built, Norfolk Southern 8664-8688 were constructed with flat-top cabs, angled radiator intakes and an overall appearance that forecast the look and configuration of their successor model, the Dash 8-40C. Departing Buffalo, N.Y., on April 23, 1989, NS 8684 and 8663 illustrate the two versions of the C39-8. The absence of air reservoirs inset with the fuel tank on the right side of the locomotive identifies the 8684 as a late C39-8, rather than a Dash 8-40C.

Union Pacific Dash 8-40C's 9133, 9126, 9210 and 9109 lead an eastbound manifest at Hermosa, Wyo., on October 23, 1988. All but 9210 are part of GE's first Dash 8-40C order, UP 9100-9174, built between November 1987 and February 1988. *William D. Miller*

	DASH 8-40C	DASH 8-40CM	DASH 8-40CW	DASH 8-44CW
Production Dates	1987-12 to 1992-12	1990-02 to 1994-03	1989-12 to 1994-11	1993-07 to 1994-03
Total Built	581	84	903	53
Length	70'8"	71'8"	70'8"	70'8"
Engine	7FDL16	7FDL16	7FDL16	7FDL16
Horsepower	4000	4000	4000	4400
Alternator	GMG 187	GMG187	GMG187	GMG187
Traction Motors	752AG	752AH	752AH	752AH
Weight x 1000 lb	400	388-395	394-400	400

DASH 8-40C

- Similar to final version of C39-8.
- Flat-top cab, roof-line flush with equipment blower and dynamic brake box.
- Angled air-intakes below oversize radiators. No step in engine hood.
- Air reservoirs mounted on right side of locomotive, below frame in recessed area of fuel tank.
- Orders built after August 1990 have dynamic brake air-intake moved to side of hood immediately behind cab.

DASH 8-40CM

- Full-cowl carbody; CN-design North American cab with four-piece windshield.

- MLW-design, Dofasco trucks.

DASH 8-40CW

- GE-design North American cab with two-piece windshield.
- Rest of locomotive similar to Dash 8-40C.
- Some late orders equipped with split cooling system, denoted by thicker radiator section.

DASH 8-44CW

- GE-design North American cab with two-piece windshield.
- Split cooling system, denoted by thicker radiator section. Otherwise similar to Dash 8-40CW.
- CSXT 9000-9052 only units built.

The transition from the C39-8 to the Dash 8-40C was an almost seamless, natural progression, with the nominal increase from 3900 to 4000 horsepower signifying more symbolic achievement than technological advance. Indeed, the most significant modifications, from software upgrades and redesign of the radiators, cooling system and dynamic brake, to carbody and cab changes, had been implemented in the final C39-8 order. Nevertheless, the introduction of the Dash 8-40C marked the Dash 8 line's coming of age.

The Dash 8-40C premiered with a 75-unit Union Pacific order in November 1987. But for the relocation of the air-reservoir tanks to a recessed position along the fuel tank on the right side of the locomotive, the original Dash 8-40C's would have been nearly indistinguishable from the late C39-8. However, the model and evolved through at least four configurations during its 7-year production run.

In its original standard-cab configuration, the Dash 8-40C sold a total of 581 units. Union Pacific, with 256 Dash 8-40C's, purchased not only the first, but the most, followed by CSX with 147, Chicago & North Western with 77, Norfolk Southern with 75 and Conrail with 25. Forecasting even bigger things to come, the last three North Western units, C&NW 8575-8577, were delivered in September 1991 rated at 4135 h.p. Furthermore, in the spring of 1992, C&NW 8543-8574 were uprated to 4150 h.p.

Canadian National commissioned a custom-designed, full-cowl version of the Dash 8-40C in 1989. Designated Dash 8-40CM, the CN units were built on trade-in MLW-Dofasco trucks from retired C630M's and featured a CN-style comfort cab with four-piece windshield, as well as the distinctive "Draper taper" in the carbody, described in reference to CN SD50F's. The first GE's sold to a Class 1 Canadian railroad since CN's 70-tonners of 1950, CN Dash 8-40CM's

Chicago & North Western Dash 8-40C 8530 and UP SD40-2 3293 return to their train at Butler, Wis., on June 14, 1999. The rooftop air-intake for the dynamic brake, visible immediately behind the cab of the locomotive, was relocated to the side of the hood (at the same location) beginning with orders built in August 1990. A number of older units have been retrofitted in the same manner.

2400-2429 were delivered in March and April 1990. By 1994, GE had delivered a total of 84 Dash 8-40CM's (all on MLW-design Dofasco trucks) to Canadian roads, including 55 to CN, 26 to BC Rail and 3 to ore-hauler Quebec North Shore & Labrador. Ironically, all three roads had once owned 70-tonners, and all went on to order GE Dash 9's.

CN's cowled Dash 8-40CM's weren't the only unusual-looking units on the shop floor at Erie in December 1989. Rubbing shoulders with the first of the CN cowls were the original examples of yet another Dash 8-40C derivative, the North American cab-equipped Dash 8-40CW. Part of a 50-unit order destined to become Union Pacific 9356-9405, the wide-nosed units were the first GE's to be built with the CN-inspired North American cab. While the full-cowl Dash 8-40CM's would be little more than a footnote in GE history, the Dash 8-40CW would soon establish a new standard and alter the look of GE diesels for years to come.

Following UP's lead, the North American cab quickly became the order of the day across the continent, and the Dash 8-40CW carried the standard, with Santa Fe, Conrail and CSX all amassing large fleets of wide-nose '40CW's in the early 1990s. In 1993, 2 years after the delivery of C&NW's uprated Dash 8-40C's, GE boosted the Dash 8-40CW's 16-FDL engine to 4135 h.p. Neither the model designation nor external appearance changed. However, some of these units, as well as some late

Working back to back, conventional and comfort cab versions of the Dash 8-40 roll through Deshler, Ohio, as CSXT Dash 8-40C 7637 and Dash 8-40CW 7896 head south with train Q501 on May 25, 2001. *William D. Miller*

Designed at the request of Canadian National, the Dash 8-40CM features a cowl carbody and CN-style comfort cab. CN took 55 of the custom cowls delivered in two orders, 2400-2429 in 1990, and 2430-2454 in 1992. All 55 ride MLW-design Dofasco trucks from C630M trade-ins. Less than two months out of Erie, CN 2419 and 2416 work through at Georgetown, Ont., on May 3, 1990.

Two other Canadian carriers took an interest in the Dash 8-40CM. Quebec North Shore & Labrador purchased a trio of the CN-inspired cowls in 1994, while BC Rail bought a total of 26 units in two orders. En route from Erie to British Columbia, BCR 4607 and 4617 pause at Toronto, Ont., on May 3, 1990.

orders rated at 4000-h.p., were equipped with GE's new split cooling system which featured thicker radiator sections. A total of 104 units, Santa Fe 927-951 and UP 9481-9559, were built with the 4135-h.p. rating.

Pushing the 16-FDL even further, and presaging the Dash 9, CSXT received 53 4400-h.p. Dash 8-44CW's in 1993-94. Other than the presence of the new split cooling system, indicated by thicker radiator sections, CSXT 9000-9052—the only Dash 8-44CW's built—are similar in appearance to their 4000-h.p. kin.

Dash 9's were already rolling off the Erie assembly lines when GE completed the final Dash 8-40CW's, all of which reverted to the original 4000 h.p. rating. Built between June and November 1994, Conrail 6230-6265 and Conrail/UP-assigned lease-fleet units LMS 700-759 closed out domestic production of the Dash 8-40C family, which, including the uprated Dash 8-44CW's, generated a total 1621 units.

Part of the first order for comfort cab GE's, UP Dash 8-40CW 9401 leads SD60M's 6243, 6156 and GP40 856 on an eastbound intermodal train at Virgilia, Calif., on November 13, 1993.

A number of late Dash 8-40CW orders were built with the split cooling system, as evidenced by the radiators of LMS 716, which are noticeably thicker than those of trailing unit C32-8 6617 at Buffalo, N.Y., on December 11, 1998.

Santa Fe westbounds pose side by side at Barstow, Calif., on February 1, 1996, offering an opportunity to compare the Dash 8-40CW and Dash 9-44CW. Heading up the stack train on the left, are Dash 8-40CW's 824, 911 and 847, while the train on the right is powered by Dash 9-44CW 647, along with SD45 5403, F45 5953 and GP20 3038. Trucks, as examination reveals, are the primary spotting difference between the six-motor Dash 8 and Dash 9 models. All C-C Dash 8's ride the Adirondack or GSC-cast truck employed by GE since the 1960s, while all six-motor Dash 9's are outfitted with GE's bolsterless HiAd trucks introduced with the model line.

CSXT Dash 8-44CW 9025 and AC4400CW 372 lead coal empties near North East, Pa., on May 15, 2000. The only Dash 8-44CW's built, CSXT 9000-9052 were constructed with the split cooling system—as indicated by the thick radiators on 9025—but are externally identical to many late Dash 8-40CW's equipped with the same feature. The absence of the rooftop air-intake for the dynamic brake, shown earlier on C&NW 8531, is evidence of the relocation of that component.

Norfolk Southern's reluctance to accept the North American cab resulted in the only Dash 9's built with conventional cabs: NS Dash 9-40C's 8764-8888, built between January and April 1995. The only conventional-cab GE's with HiAd trucks, the Dash 9-40C's are readily distinguishable from their Dash 8 kin, as illustrated by NS 8796 at SK Yard in Buffalo, N.Y., on September 19, 1995. *William D. Miller*

DASH 9-40C
- HiAd, bolsterless trucks.
- 2 ½ feet longer than Dash 8-40C.
- Split cooling system, as indicated by thicker radiator section.
- Hand brake centered below radiators.
- Carbody design and configuration otherwise similar to Dash 8-40C.
- NS 8764-8888 only units built.

DASH 9-40CW
- North American cab.
- HiAd, bolsterless trucks.
- 2 ½ feet longer than Dash 8-40CW.
- Split cooling system, as indicated by thicker radiator section.
- Hand brake centered below radiators.
- Carbody design and configuration otherwise similar to Dash 8-40CW.
- NS 8889-9744 only units built.

DASH 9-44CW
- Identical to Dash 9-40CW

DASH 9-44CWL
- CN-design North American cab with four-piece windshield.
- 6 inches longer than Dash 9-44CW.
- CN 2500-2522, BC Rail 4641-4644 only units built.

	DASH 9-40C	DASH 9-40CW	DASH 9-44CW	DASH 9-44CWL
Production Dates	1995-01 to 1995-04	1996-01 to current	1993-11 to current	1994-12 to 1995-03
Total Built	120	856	1768	27
Length	73'2"	73'2"	73'2"	73'8"
Engine	7FDL16	7FDL16	7FDL16	7FDL16
Horsepower	4000	4000	4400	4400
Alternator	GMG197	GMG197	GMG197	GMG197
Traction Motors	752AH	752AH	752AH	752AH
Weight x 1000 lb	410	410	400	385

The continuing evolution of the third-generation General Electric locomotive reached a new plateau as GE's Dash 8 series gave way to the Dash 9 in 1993. Conspicuous by its absence from the new Dash 9 catalog was a four-motor freight model. It was a sign of the industry's near insatiable appetite for nothing but high-horsepower C-C's that GE neither offered nor was asked for a B-B, Dash 9 freight locomotive. The cornerstone of the new line was— and is—the 4400-h.p., 6-motor, Dash 9-44CW.

Slightly longer than its Dash 8 predecessor, the Dash 9-44CW is built on a 73-foot, 2-inch platform that is shared with its A.C. traction counterpart, the AC4400CW. GE's HiAd truck, a bolsterless, low-weight-transfer truck designed for improved adhesion, was introduced with the Dash 9-44CW. The new truck, combined with enhanced, microprocessor-driven, wheel-slip control, allows the Dash 9-44CW to boast all-weather adhesion as high as 30 percent.

Norfolk Southern finally adopted the industry-standard North American cab in 1996, but has continued to opt for a 4000-h.p. rating on its Dash 9's. Formally designated Dash 9-40CW, the 4000 h.p. locomotives are virtually identical to the 4400-h.p. Dash 9-44CW, as shown by NS 9032 at St. Thomas, Ont., on April 28, 2000. NS has been the sole customer for the Dash 9-40CW and has thus far purchased a total of 856 units, numbered 8889-9744.

Most of the Dash 9 Series improvements were internal, and many had been tested and or perfected on Dash 8 locomotives. The split cooling system, evidenced by thicker radiator sections, and designed to reduce engine inlet air temperatures and thus improve fuel economy, lower emissions and extend engine life, became a standard Dash 9 feature. Other Dash 8 options such as computerized Integrated Function Control, electronic fuel injection and on-board diagnostics became commonplace, if not standard, Dash 9 equipment.

More than 2700 six-motor Dash 9's have emerged from Erie since

Chicago & North Western took delivery of the first Dash 9-44CW's in November 1993. With the exception of minor railroad-specified options such as headlight and numberboard placement, most are similar in appearance to the first Dash 9, Chicago & North Western 8601. There are, however, several variations.

Norfolk Southern, resistant to the North American cab and accompanying console control stand, as well as the 4400-h.p. rating of the Dash 9-44CW, ordered 120 Dash 9-40C's outfitted with standard cabs and AAR control stands. Delivered between January and April 1995, NS 8764-8888 were the last domestic GE's constructed with standard cabs. The only Dash 9-40C's built, they can be distinguished from Dash 8-40C's by their HiAd trucks and split cooling radiators, with the hand brake centered beneath them. The units are capable of being uprated to 4400 h.p. through high-level computer functions and fuel rack adjustments.

Although NS has since embraced the North American cab, Roanoke has insisted upon retaining conventional control stands and the 4000-h.p. rating on subsequent Dash 9 orders. The 4000-h.p. Dash 9-40CW, with its North American cab and conventional control stand is a model unique to NS, but the road has made it worth GE's while and has thus far purchased 856 such units. The NS Dash 9-40CW's are outwardly identical to Dash 9-44CW's and, in fact, are capable of being uprated to 4400 h.p. through high-level internal computer functions and adjustment of fuel-rack settings.

Trucks are the primary spotting difference between six-motor Dash 8 and Dash 9 series locomotives, a fact well illustrated as Santa Fe Dash 8-40CW 824 and Dash 9-44CW 647 pose side by side at Barstow, Calif., on February 1, 1996. Santa Fe 824, like all C-C Dash 8's, rides on the Adirondack or GSC-cast three-axle truck employed by GE since the 1960s. Meanwhile, all six-motor Dash 9's ride GE's new bolsterless HiAd trucks introduced with the model line. The GSC/Adirondack and HiAd trucks are not interchangeable, however, the HiAd truck is also found on many GE A.C. locomotives.

Showing off the distinctive paint scheme designed specifically for their class, Chicago & North Western Dash 9-44CW's 8682 and 8658 bask in the sun at Missouri Valley, Iowa, on May 12, 1995. North Western took delivery of the first Dash 9-44CW's, C&NW 8601-8635, in November-December 1993 and amassed a fleet of 130 of the 4400-h.p. units within 6 months.

As it had with the Dash 8, Canadian National specified its own version of the Dash 9-44CW, but opted for a standard hood-unit design. Designated Dash 9-44CWL, CN 2500-2522 were built in December 1994 on a slightly longer platform and equipped with the CN version of the wide-nose comfort cab with its distinctive four-piece windshield. BC Rail followed suit several months later, taking four of its own Dash 9-44CWL's outfitted with the CN cab. In later Dash 9 orders, both BC Rail and CN bowed to standardization and accepted standard GE North American cabs on subsequent Dash 9-44CW orders.

The six-motor Dash 9 has also found success beyond North America, from Dash 9-44CW's on Australia's Hamersley Iron and its successor Pilbra Railways, to 5-foot, 3-inch gauge versions hauling ore in Brazil for E.F. Carjas and meter gauge B+B-B+B Dash 9-40BBW's working for Brazilian mineral hauler Vitoria a Minas.

After purchasing 55 customized, full-cowl Dash 8-40CM's, Canadian National reverted to stock hood units for its first Dash 9 order, but again specified its own cab. Designated Dash 9-44CWL, CN 2500-2522 were built in December 1994 on platforms 6 inches longer than the standard Dash 9 frame and equipped with CN's own version of the North American cab, featuring a four-piece windshield. BC Rail 4641-4644, built to CN specs in March 1995, are the only other Dash 9-44CWL's in existence.

Following the CWL order, CN finally opted for a stock GE model, taking 120 Dash 9-44CW's with the standard GE North American cab, albeit with customized windshields patterned after the version ordered by Australia's Hamersley Iron. As shown by Dash 9-44CW 2581, the lower lines of the windshields on the CN units follow the contour of the nose in an effort to improve visibility.

Southern Pacific's last new locomotives were Dash 9-44CW's 8100-8200, delivered between April and December 1994. In the employ of Union Pacific, SP Dash 9-44CW 8169 is still in factory-applied Espee paint at Daggett, Calif., on November 26, 1997.

To meet clearance restrictions, primarily at the York Canyon, N. Mex., coal loadout, Santa Fe specified a unique notched cab roof on its Dash 8-40CW's and Dash 9-44CW's. Standing at GE's back gate in Erie, Pa., on August 5, 1997, brand-new BNSF Dash 9-44CW's 725 and 727 exhibit the so-called "gull wing" cab roof, a specification that BNSF has continued to order on all of its GE's.

GE's first A.C. traction locomotive, AC4400CW testbed 2000 works out on the test track east of Erie, Pa., with UP AC6000CW 7510 on May 19, 1998. The 2000 was built with MLW-style Dofasco trucks and is the only GE A.C. locomotive so equipped.

	AC4400CW
Production Dates	1993-06 to current
Total Built	2249
Length	73'2"
Engine	7FDL16
Horsepower	4400
Alternator	GMG196A
Traction Motors	GEB13
Weight x 1000 lb	420

AC4400CW

- North American cab.
- HiAd, bolsterless trucks; GE steerable trucks optional on later models.
- Large box behind cab on left side of locomotive—contains inverter banks and A.C. traction circuitry.
- Vented access panels beneath the cab on the right side of locomotive.
- Otherwise externally similar to Dash 9-44CW.

Generally Electric entered the A.C. traction locomotive business two steps behind the competition, but regained lost ground at a rapid pace. While EMD investigated the concept and fielded A.C. traction test units and prototypes in the late 1980s and early 1990s, GE waited in the wings. However, when it became apparent that A.C. drive would be both practical and marketable, Erie wasted no time in producing an A.C. traction locomotive of its own. In June 1993, just 2 years after EMD's first SD60MAC testbeds hit the road, GE outshopped its first A.C. traction locomotive, AC4400CW prototype No. 2000. A year later, the first production AC4400CW's, CSXT 9100-9102, were delivered from Erie.

The AC4400CW is basically an A.C. traction version of the Dash 9-44CW. The overall appearance of the AC4400 is very similar to that of its Dash 9 counterpart, with the exception of a large box behind the operator cab on the left side of the locomotive. This box, found on all General Electric A.C.

The large box behind the cab of CP 8562 immediately identifies the locomotive as an AC4400CW. Found on the left side of all General Electric A.C. freight locomotives, this box forms the back wall of the electrical cabinet containing the inverter banks and much of the A.C. traction circuitry. Seen at Moose Jaw, Sask., on December 6, 1998, CP 8562 and 8573 are outfitted with GE's optional steerable truck.

freight locomotives, forms the outer (left) side of the inverter cabinet containing the inverter banks and much of the A.C. traction circuitry. On the right side of the locomotive, vented access panels beneath the cab offer the only subtle evidence that the locomotive is an A.C. rather than a Dash 9.

There are a number of differences between the GE and EMD A.C.

traction control systems and inverter packages. Most fundamental is GE's use of one inverter bank per traction motor, versus EMD's application, which uses one inverter bank per truck. The GE design allows individual traction motors to be cut out in the event of problems, whereas EMD locomotives must have the entire truck cut out in order to isolate a problem motor.

On the right side, the AC4400CW is nearly identical to the Dash 9-44CW, as shown by SP AC4400CW 208 at Mojave, Calif., on February 4, 1996. The vented access panels beneath the cab of the 208 identify the locomotive as an A.C.

Inverter banks, each of which consists of six GTO's (Gated Turn On devices), or IGBT's (Integrated Gate Bipolar Transistors) starting in early 1998, chop D.C. power from the main alternator to three-phase A.C. power, which is delivered to the traction motors. Erie's decision to employ one inverter per traction motor gives GE A.C.'s a massive wall of 36 GTO's in six inverter banks contained in the distinctive box on the left side of the locomotive.

Although GE came late to the A.C. party, the Erie-built A.C. locomotives have outsold those of EMD. However, EMD's HTCR-II radial truck was generally regarded as superior to the GE HiAd employed beneath the AC4400CW. To address the issue, GE developed its own steerable truck to compete with the HTCR. The new truck made its appearance in 1996 and has been used on a number of AC4400 orders constructed since then. However, some roads, notably Union Pacific, have stuck with the "non-radial" HiAd truck on GE A.C.'s.

One of 35 Chicago & North Western AC4400CW's, CNW 8805 leads a loaded coal train over Logan Hill in Wyoming's Powder River Basin on March 30, 1997.

An overhead view of UP AC4400CW 6869 illustrates the immense bulk of the A.C. electrical cabinet. The presence of this box displaced the cab air-conditioning equipment from the left-side gangway to an area beneath the cab floor on A.C. locomotives, as seen on UP 6869.

One of 14 preproduction AC6000CW testbeds outshopped in December 1995, GE 6000 is assigned to GE's Erie, Pa., test fleet.

AC6000CW

- North American cab.
- Large radiators overhanging sides and rear of hood.
- Large box behind cab on left side of locomotive—contains inverter banks and A.C. traction circuitry.
- Two square exhaust stacks, indicating twin-turbo, 6000-h.p., 7HDL engine.
- Engine hood profiled with square edges.
- Walkway stepped to clear air reservoirs above fuel tank on right side.
- HiAd, bolsterless trucks or GE steerable trucks.

AC6000CW Upgradable (C6044AC)

- Single exhaust, indicating 4400-h.p. FDL16 engine. Otherwise identical to 6000-h.p. version.
- HiAd, bolsterless trucks.
- GE 4400, UP 7010-7079, 7300-7335 only units built.

	AC6000CW	AC6000CW (Upgradable)
Production Dates	1995-12 to current	1995-08 to 1998-04
Total Built	198	107
Length	76'0"	76'0"
Engine	7FDL16	7FDL16
Horsepower	6000	4400
Alternator	GMG201	GMG201
Traction Motors	GEB13	GEB13
Weight x 1000 lb	425	412

In partnership with Deutz MWM of Mannheim, Germany, GE worked to develop and perfect the 16-cylinder, 250mm-bore, 320mm-stroke 7HDL16A prime mover as the power plant for the 6000-h.p., A.C. traction AC6000CW. As an essential element of the development program, Erie built 14 preproduction, HDL-powered prototypes in 1995: GE 6000, CSXT 600-602 and Union Pacific 7000-7009.

Constructed on a 76-foot platform and riding HiAd trucks, the 6000-h.p. units were outfitted with huge radiators and massive 5500-gallon fuel tanks to satisfy the cooling demands and appetite of the HDL engine. The size of the fuel tanks pushed the air reservoirs to a higher position, making a step in the right-side walkway necessary, while the oversize radiators extended beyond the rear of the hood, giving the locomotive an even larger presence.

While the testbeds hit the road to gather essential in-service performance data and experience, GE began

Working the test track east of Erie, Pa., on May 19, 1998, UP 7510, the first production model AC6000CW, teams up with GE AC4400CW 2000, the first GE A.C. traction locomotive.

building "convertible" AC6000CW's outfitted with stock 4400-h.p. FDL16 engines. Primer-grey GE testbed 4400 was outshopped in August 1995, while the first UP convertibles began emerging from Erie in November. Intended to be retrofitted with HDL's when the new engine was perfected, the C6044AC's, as UP has dubbed

them, are fully capable of supporting the 6000-h.p. prime mover when— or if—the transplant program is effected. GE makes no distinction between the convertibles and the 6000-h.p. AC6000CW's on the builder's decals, and the two versions are outwardly identical.

The only road to purchase

convertible versions of the AC6000CW, UP has accumulated a fleet of 106 C6044AC's, along with 80 HDL-powered, "true" AC6000CW's. One of these, UP 7511, is a replacement, the original having been damaged by fire and replaced by GE. The former UP 7511, meanwhile, has been rebuilt and serves in the Erie test fleet as GECX 6002.

Although UP has long held the reputation of champion of the high-horsepower set, CSXT has quietly assembled an impressive AC6000CW fleet of its own. Including the three original testbeds, CSXT has purchased a total of 117 HDL-powered AC6000CW's. While UP continues spec the HiAd truck, CSXT's AC6000's ride on GE's steerable truck.

Thus far, UP and CSXT have been the only domestic customers for the AC6000CW, but in 1998-99, Erie exported eight HDL-powered AC60's to Australia's Pilbra mining region in the employ of BHP Iron Ore.

General Electric makes no formal distinction between the 6000-h.p. AC6000CW and its upgradable 4400-h.p. counterpart. However, to avoid confusion, Union Pacific, the only road to purchase the "convertible" version, designates the 4400-h.p. units C6044AC. Offering an opportunity to compare versions, UP C6044AC 7040 leads AC6000CW's 7508 and 7532 out of West Colton, Calif., on April 3, 1999. The single exhaust stack of UP 7040's 16-cylinder FDL engine, compared to the twin stacks of the 6000-h.p. HDL engines in Nos. 7508 and 7532, is the only obvious difference between the 4400-h.p. upgradable and the full-fledged 6000-h.p. AC6000CW. All UP AC6000CW's and C6044AC's ride on HiAd trucks.

To satisfy the cooling requirements of the 6000-h.p. HDL engine, the AC6000CW is outfitted with enormous radiators that give the already impressive locomotive an even greater presence. At Blasdell, N.Y., on May 15, 2000, CSXT 677, one of the road's 117 AC6000CW's shows off the distinctive rads that make the model instantly identifiable. All CSXT AC6000CW's are equipped with steerable trucks.

Part of the first Amtrak order for Genesis Series 1 locomotives, Dash 8-40BP 826 leads Dash 8-32BWH 503 through Lugo, Calif., on February 2, 1996.

	DASH 8-40BP	P32AC-DM	P42DC
Production Dates	1993-03 to 1993-04	1995-04 to current	1996-08 to current
Total Built	46	53	228
Length	69'0"	69'0"	69'0"
Engine	7FDL16	7FDL12	7FDL16
Horsepower	4000	3200	4200
Alternator	GMG195 (Traction) GTA33A1 (HEP)	GMG195A1 (Traction)	GMG195 (Traction) GTA33 (HEP)
Traction Motors	752AH8	GEB15	752AH
Weight x 1000 lb	262.8	274.4	266

DASH 8-40BP
- Streamlined, Genesis Series monocoque carbody.
- German-design bolsterless trucks; hydraulic shocks and flexicoil suspension.

P32AC-DM
- Same Genesis Series carbody as Dash 8-40BP, but additional ventilation openings for A.C. traction and dual-mode equipment.

- German-design bolsterless trucks; hydraulic shocks and flexicoil suspension.
- Dual-mode; retractable pickup shoes for third-rail electric operation.

P42DC
- Streamlined, Genesis Series monocoque carbody.
- Externally identical to Dash 8-40BP.

G eneral Electric scored a major
coup with the 1991 award of
an Amtrak contract to supply the
passenger carrier with a total of 52
units. The first 20 units of the order
were the previously mentioned Dash
8-32BWH model, but the balance of
the order was for an entirely new
breed of passenger locomotive, the
Genesis.

Amtrak handed GE a tough set of
specifications for its new-generation
passenger locomotive, calling for
a microprocessor-controlled,
HEP-equipped, 4000-h.p. locomotive
that weighed less than the 3000-h.p.
F40; it also had to squeeze through
Hudson River tunnels, deliver HEP at
a lower engine speed while standing
at stations, and be adaptable to a
dual-mode, diesel-electric/electric in
future versions. GE's response was
Dash 8-40BP.

Fashioned in collaboration
with GE's German affiliate, Krupp
Verkehrstechnik GMBH, the Dash
8-40BP rides on high-speed, German-
design bolsterless trucks equipped

Amtrak P42DC 52 represents the latest version of the Genesis Series 1 passenger locomotive, an internally upgraded model that is externally identical to the Dash 8-40BP.

with hydraulic shocks and flexicoil
suspension, and packs a 4000-h.p.,
FDL16 engine and 800KW, 480VAC,
three-phase, 60-cycle, GTA33A1 HEP
alternator in its sleek monocoque
carbody. Equipped with microprocessor controls, Integrated Function
Control, Micro-Sentry wheel-slip
control and blended braking, Amtrak
800-845 were delivered in March-
April 1993. Figuratively—and literally
—the 800's were the shape of things
to come.

The second wave of Genesis
locomotives came in the form of
A.C. traction, dual-mode P32AC-DM's.

Designed for New York-area passenger duty, the P32AC-DM is capable of operating as a conventional diesel-electric or as a straight electric, drawing power from the 650-volt D.C. third rail in electrified territory in and out of New York City's Grand Central Terminal and Pennsylvania Station.

Making use of the same Genesis carbody as the Dash 8-40BP, the P32AC-DM combines a 3200-h.p., 12-cylinder FDL prime mover with a 4-motor A.C. propulsion package. As with other GE A.C.'s, the P32AC-DM is set up with one inverter bank per traction motor, with a fifth inverter functioning in concert with the locomotive's 800kW HEP alternator. As protection, the locomotive's No. 1 traction inverter provides automatic backup to the HEP inverter.

Amtrak, Metro North and the Connecticut Department of Transportation have all purchased P32AC-DM's for passenger and commuter duty in the New York region.

Successor to the Dash 8-40BP, the 4200-h.p. P42DC is the latest version

Dual-mode P32AC-DM's Amtrak 709 and Metro North 201 undergo third-rail testing at GE in Erie, Pa., on September 6, 1995.

of the Genesis Series passenger locomotive. The P42DC retains the original carbody, but beneath its monocoque skin, the engine, electronics and microprocessor controls of the locomotive have been redesigned and upgraded. Enhanced with such features such as electronic fuel injection, micro-computer-based integrated control, full on-board diagnostics and even

remote engine starting, the P42DC has become the backbone of the Amtrak fleet, all but replacing the F40PH.

Since the model's introduction in 1996, Amtrak has purchased 207 P42DC's and, until recently, had been the only customer for the model. However, in late 2001, VIA began taking delivery of 21 P42DC's, its first GE diesels.

Connecticut Department of Transportation's four P32AC-DM's were delivered in 2001 wearing a striking adaptation of the New Haven's famed "McGinnis" paint scheme. Front and rear views show newly delivered No. 228 at Harmon, N.Y., on October 13, 2001, along with No. 231—the last unit of the order—at New Haven, Conn., on December 16, 2001. *Scott A. Hartley*

Fresh from the paint shop, Santa Fe GP60M's 116 and 120 idle outside the test house at General Motors Diesel in London, Ont., on June 15, 1990.

General Motors Electro-Motive Division

North America's number-one locomotive builder from 1945 until 1983, General Motors' Electro-Motive Division has undergone dramatic changes in recent times. In 1988, EMD shut down the locomotive assembly lines at its legendary La Grange, Ill., facility—"Home of the Diesel Locomotive" since 1936—and shifted production to its Diesel Division subsidiary in London, Ontario.

The 3.6-million-square-foot EMD plant, which occupied a sprawling acreage in the Chicago suburb of McCook, but took its name from its La Grange postal address, turned out its first locomotives in 1936 and ended full production in 1988. The last La Grange-built locomotive of all, Metra F40PHM-2 214, was outshopped in December 1992.

However, the La Grange facility remains home to EMD's corporate headquarters and continues to produce certain major components, including prime movers.

In the spring of 2000, the Main Plant, High Bay and other Locomotive Division buildings at La Grange were demolished, following two all-but-forgotten EMD plants into history. Plant No. 2, a former Pullman Company facility on Chicago's South Side, was set up in 1946 to produce switcher underframes, cab assemblies for E's, F's and Geeps, as well as numerous subassemblies, components and sheet-metal fabrications. Its functions gradually farmed out or moved to La Grange, Plant 2 closed in the late 1980s.

Located in Electro-Motive's old hometown of Cleveland, Ohio, Plant

UP SD90MAC-H 8205 receives finishing touches in the Desnag Department at London on May 1, 1997.

Builder's plate, UP SD90MAC-H 8205.

Almost ready for paint, UP SD90MAC's 8152 and 8150 stand on the shop floor at London on May 1, 1997. The dynamic brake fan on 8150 fills the bottom right corner of the image.

La Grange in late 1987 with an order for 20 Southern Pacific GP60's. Shortly thereafter, London assumed its new role as the main locomotive assembly facility for the General Motors Locomotive Group. Initially, London was able to handle the increased workload, however, a rebound in locomotive orders soon pushed volume well beyond the limit of its capacity to outshop one-and-one-half units per day.

In 1994-95, in an effort to relieve the backlog at London and increase overall production capacity, 45 Conrail SD60I's were shipped in "kit" form to the road's Juniata shop in Altoona, Pa., for final assembly and paint. The concept of contracting locomotive assembly to outside shops caught on, and EMD has come to rely heavily on outside shops to assemble new locomotives from "kits" supplied by the builder.

Under the Conrail flag, the Juniata shop went on to assemble 24 CR SD70's and 15 SD70MAC's, along with 16 more '70MAC's for BNSF. Several more orders of EMD

No. 3 was established in 1948 to handle overflow production during the heyday of early dieselization. An estimated 3614 SW-series switchers, GP7's and GP9's were built in Cleveland before Plant 3 closed its doors in 1954. To the chagrin of diesel historians, there are few, if any, known records detailing the actual identities of Cleveland-built EMD's.

Opened in 1950 as General Motors Diesel Ltd., the London plant was established to serve Canadian and export markets. The relatively small facility began taking on work from kits have rolled out of Juniata since Norfolk Southern took over the shop with its share of the Conrail assets in 1999, including 16 Alaska SD70MAC's, 14 CEFX SD9043MAC's and 10 of the road's own SD70M's.

Two facilities in particular have come to play a major role in the assembly of EMD locomotives. Longtime EMD supplier Super Steel's Glenville, N.Y., facility, known as Super Steel Schenectady Inc., was established in 1994 to meet the New York content requirements in the contract to build DE30AC and DM30AC commuter locomotives for the Long Island Railroad.

SSSI has assembled far more than just the 46 Long Island locomotives, though. The New York plant has become a key EMD assembly facility and has thus far turned out more than 200 locomotives, including IC SD70's, UP SD70M's, BNSF SD70MAC's, UP SD90MAC-H II's and CEFX SD9043MAC's. Passenger locomotives have become an SSSI specialty, and the Glenville shop has handled almost all F59PHI's built for the U.S. market since 1998. Most of

UP SD90MAC-H 8203 and SD90MAC's 8107 and 8104 near completion at London on March 5, 1997.

the locomotives assembled at Super Steel have been outshopped in primer and shipped to Alstom's Hornell, N.Y., shop for paint.

South of the border, Bombardier-Concarril's plant in Sahagun, Mexico, has proven to be EMD's most productive contractor. Hundreds of new EMD locomotives have

rolled off the Concarril assembly line since the plant completed its first unit, BNSF SD70MAC 9866, in April 1998. In fewer than 3 years, Bombardier-Concarril has outshopped at least 246 BNSF SD70MAC's and 124 UP SD70M's, along with 75 SD70MAC's for Kansas City Southern's

Still dressed in primer, UP SD90MAC's 8007 and 8004 get a workout on GMD's London, Ont., test track on January 12, 1996.

Mexican subsidiary Transportacion Ferroviaria Mexicana (TFM).

In Canada, CP's Ogden Shop in Calgary, Alta., assembled 49 of the road's SD9043MAC's (and painted all 61 units in the order), while Alstom's former Pointe St. Charles shop in Montreal, Que., has assembled 35 CN SD75I's, 6 SD75I's for Ontario Northland and 11 F59PHI's for Montreal-area commuter agency Agence Metropolitaine de Transport.

Despite the volume of off-site assembly, London prevails as EMD's primary production facility, building locomotives for the North American and export markets. From locomotive frames to cabs, control stands, trucks and traction motors, London fabricates many of the components for not only the units it builds but also for the assembly kits shipped to contract shops.

La Grange may no longer build locomotives, but the home of the diesel locomotive continues to produce a number of major components, including electrical equipment and high-voltage cabinets, radiators and the associated hood sections, turbochargers and prime movers.

The concept of EMD locomotives being produced in five separate locations—and none of them La Grange—may at first seem unusual. However, the practice harks back to the company's humble beginnings in a Cleveland warehouse in 1922. With no factory of its own, Electro-Motive contracted railroad shops and car-builders to assemble the self-propelled, gas-electric passenger and combination cars that gave the fledgling company its start.

Even after General Motors' 1930 purchase of Electro-Motive and its principal supplier, the Winton Engine Co., the pioneer builder continued to employ outside shops. The future site of the La Grange locomotive plant was still an open field when, in early 1934, Electro-Motive charted the course of history with the first railroad application of its original diesel power plant. The future of railroading worldwide was changed forever as workers at the E.G. Budd Manufacturing Company in Philadelphia lowered an eight-cylinder, 600-h.p. Winton 201A diesel into the power car of the Burlington Zephyr under construction at the Red Lion works.

Electro-Motive's first diesel locomotives, a pair of Winton-powered boxcab testbeds and two SC-model switchers for the Lackawanna, were also constructed under contract by outside shops in 1935. Ironically, the four locomotives were built in the Erie, Pa., works of future competitor General Electric.

SOO SD60 6052 poses for the company photographer, while sister 6054 (with incomplete lettering) takes a spin on the test track at London on October 25, 1989.

Furthermore, most Electro-Motive gas-cars, as well as its early locomotives, were outfitted with GE electrical equipment. Indeed, EMD's entire line of D.C. traction motors are based on the GE motors first slung on the trucks of its locomotives in 1938.

Tens of thousands of locomotives later, the name Electro-Motive remains synonymous with the North American diesel locomotive. Whether built in La Grange or London, Montreal or Altoona, Cleveland, Concarril or Calgary, all EMD's share a common bond, a connection to "the home of the diesel locomotive," and a link to a simple, two-story warehouse in Cleveland.

Electro-Motive SD90MAC-H
Location of Equipment

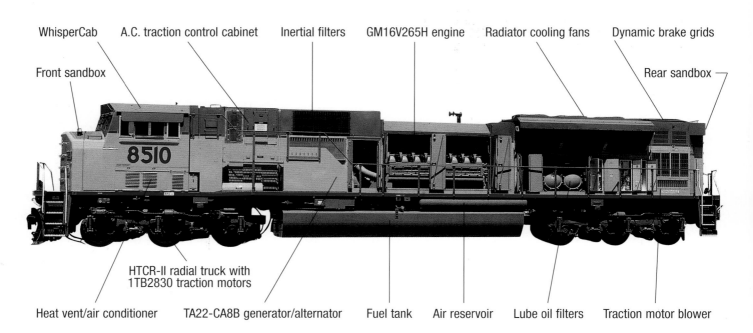

WhisperCab

A.C. traction control cabinet

Inertial filters

GM16V265H engine

Radiator cooling fans

Dynamic brake grids

Front sandbox

Rear sandbox

8510

HTCR-II radial truck with
1TB2830 traction motors

Heat vent/air conditioner

TA22-CA8B generator/alternator

Fuel tank

Air reservoir

Lube oil filters

Traction motor blower

Blomberg

HT-B

HT-C

HTCR-II

Bolsterless (with third-rail pickup shoe)

MODEL	8-645E	12-645E	16-645E/F	20-645E
Cylinders	8	12	16	20
Maximum RPM	900	900	900	900-950
Stroke Cycle	2	2	2	2
Bore/Stroke	9 1/16" x 10"	9 1/16" x 10"	9 1/16" x 10"	9 1/16" x 10"
H.P. / Roots-blown	1000	1500	2000	NA
H.P. / Turbocharged	1500	2300	3000-3500	3600

MODEL	12-710GB	16-710GB	20-710GB	16-265H
Cylinders	12	16	20	16
Maximum RPM	950	950	950	1000
Stroke Cycle	2	2	2	4
Bore/Stroke	9 1/16" x 11"	9 1/16" x 11"	9 1/16" x 11"	265 x 300 mm
H.P. / Turbocharged	3000	3800-4300	5000	6000

16-265H

The easy beat of a two-cycle engine has been the trademark sound of Electro-Motive diesels since the introduction of the Winton 201A in the early 1930s. From the eight-cylinder in-line 201A installed in the Burlington Zephyr of 1934, through its 567 and 645 series successors, to the V-20, 5000-h.p., 710G3B prime mover in the SD80MAC, EMD has remained true to the two-cycle concept.

The 710 series engine remains in production, in 12-, 16- and 20-cylinder versions, as the power plant for everything from the F59PHI to the SD80MAC. However, in 1994, EMD stepped away from the two-cycle standard. In need of an engine capable of producing the 6000-h.p. rating of the SD90MAC, EMD designers turned to four-cycle power.

The most powerful EMD prime mover ever, the four-cycle 16V265H engine produces a record 394 b.h.p. (brake horsepower) per cylinder—50 percent more than the 16-710—with 30 percent fewer parts than its two-cycle predecessor. The performance of the 6000-h.p. (6300 b.h.p.) H-engine is enhanced by a number of innovative design features, including twin-turbochargers, one centrally located camshaft, newly developed Thermo-flex (patented and copyrighted) crown pistons and a cross-flow cylinder head designed to provide more complete combustion, improve fuel efficiency and reduce emissions.

While previous EMD prime movers, including the 710, have utilized fabricated steel crankcases, the 265H engine is constructed with a one-piece ductile cast-iron crankcase in an effort to increase structural strength and reduce vibration. Further separating the 265H from its two-cycle kin is its capacity to use antifreeze in its

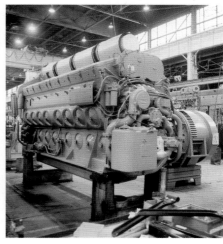

16-710GB

cooling system, permitting the locomotive to be shut down in cold weather without the need to drain the coolant. However, like all EMD engines, the 16V265H is designed and built in La Grange.

One of a declining number of end-cab switchers in the employ of Class 1 railroads, freshly painted BNSF SW1000 3636 idles at Superior, Wis., on September 28, 2000. The SW1000 and SW1500 share the same carbody, but the SW1000's single exhaust stack makes it easily identifiable.

	SW1000	SW1001	SW1500	SW1504
Production Dates	1966-06 to 1972-10	1968-09 to 1986-06	1966-07 to 1974-01	1973-05 to 1973-08
Total Built	118	174	808	60
Length	44'8"	44'8"	44'8"	46'8"
Engine	8-645E	8-645E	12-645E	12-645E
Horsepower	1000	1000	1500	1500
Alternator	D25	D25	D32	D32
Traction Motors	D77	D77	D77	D77
Weight x 1000 lb	240-260	230	248-260	219

SW1000
- Same carbody as SW1500, but single exhaust stack for 8-645 engine.
- AAR type A switcher trucks standard, Flexicoil optional.

SW1001
- Same hood as SW1000—single exhaust stack.
- Low-clearance cab; 14-foot, 3-inch overall height vs 15 feet for SW1000/SW1500.
- Frame and walkway lower; frame end-plates higher than walkway.
- AAR type A switcher trucks, Flexicoil optional.

SW1500
- Same carbody as SW1000, but two exhaust stacks for 12-645 engine.
- Larger radiator section than SW1000 and SW1001.
- AAR type A switcher trucks or Flexicoil.
- More than half built with Flexicoil trucks.

SW1504
- Similar to MP15DC, but for louvered air-filter box ahead of cab.
- Blomberg trucks.
- NdeM 8800-8859 only units built.

Tracing its roots to the six-cylinder, 600-h.p. SW1 introduced in January 1939, EMD's famed "SW" line of switchers culminated with the 1966 debut of the 645-powered SW1000 and SW1500. The standard EMD switcher carbody was redesigned for the new model line, with a higher cab, less-rounded cab roof and a boxier hood. Hood-top radiators at the front of the locomotive, once barely visible, were more exposed—covered only by a steel grille that extended several inches down the side of the hood as well. Protecting the radiator fan shutters at the very front of the locomotive, a similar grille replaced the steel mesh used on earlier SW models. Topping off the redesigned hood, the headlight and numberboards, which were previously combined as a single component, were incorporated into a sheetmetal housing resembling a scaled-down version of the housing found on the Canadian-built SW1200RS and GMD1.

Although they share the same

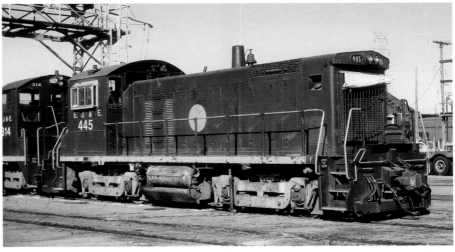

Elgin Joliet & Eastern SW1001 445, at Gary, Ind., on January 15, 1996, exhibits the low-clearance cab and low walkways that distinguish the model from the SW1000. Essentially a low-profile version of the SW1000, the SW1001 became the sole 1000-h.p. switcher in EMD's catalog after 1972 and remained in production until mid-1986. *Mark R. Lynn*

carbody, the SW1000 and SW1500 can be readily differentiated; the 1000-h.p., 8-cylinder engine in the SW1000 has a single exhaust stack, versus the twin exhaust stacks of the 12-cylinder, 1500-h.p. prime mover in the SW1500.

Riding noticeably higher than their predecessors, the new SW's were, in fact, too tall for the tight clearances found on the trackage of many industrial operations. As a result, EMD added the SW1001 to its switcher lineup in 1968. Essentially a low-profile version of the SW1000, the SW1001 featured a lower frame-height as well as a shorter, low-clearance cab that reduced the overall clearance requirements of the locomotive, but increased its marketability. To simplify the product line, EMD dropped the SW1000 from its catalog with the introduction of the Dash 2 line in the fall of 1972, but continued to offer—and produce—the SW1001 until mid-1986.

As with previous switcher models, EMD offered the SW1000, SW1001 and SW1500 on either the traditional AAR type A switcher trucks, or the optional Flexicoil truck. While most of the SW1000/1001's were built with type A's, at least 418 SW1500's—more than half the 808 built—were delivered riding Flexicoil trucks.

EMD's most powerful switcher at the time, the SW1500 found favor among a number of railroads as a heavy-duty yard engine, transfer locomotive and road-switcher. In fact, Southern Pacific, with 240, and Penn Central, with 112 (including 28 on Chicagoland subsidiary Indiana Harbor Belt), accounted for nearly half the total production.

The SW1500 was available on AAR type A switcher trucks or Flexicoil trucks. Riding plain-bearing switcher trucks, TRRA SW1500 1506 idles at Brooklyn, Ill., on July 9, 1981. *David R. Busse*

In common with more than half of the 808 SW1500's built, Illinois Terminal 1510, seen at Madison, Ill., on December 19, 1976, is equipped with Flexicoil trucks. *David R. Busse*

Custom-built for Nacionales de Mexico, the SW1504 sports a distinctive louvered air-filter box ahead of the cab and rides Blomberg trucks. Dressed in FNM's two-tone blue scheme, but still carrying its original NdeM road number, SW1504 8811 basks in the sun at Torrcon, Mexico, on February 13, 2000. *Paul Wester, Mark R. Lynn collection*

However popular, the locomotive's ability to perform in road service was handicapped by its relatively light weight and the inability to accommodate the Blomberg road truck due to its short frame-length. In an effort to surmount at least one of these shortcomings, Nacionales de Mexico ordered the custom-built SW1504. With a frame 2 feet longer than that of the SW1500, the SW1504 rode on Blomberg trucks, but weighed in at just 219,000 pounds, considerably lighter than the 248,000-260,000-lb., SW1500. Further distinguished from the SW1500 by a large, louvered air-filter box located on the upper portion of the engine hood between the cab and second exhaust stack, the 60 SW1504's (the only ones built) delivered to NdeM between May and August 1973 presaged the MP15, which would be introduced just 6 months later.

Blomberg trucks and a low-profile air-filter box ahead of the cab identify Manufacturers Railway 252, at St. Louis, Mo., on January 4, 1976, as an MP15DC. Most, but not all, MP15DC's are equipped with the filter box; all are on Blomberg trucks. *David R. Busse*

	MP15DC	MP15AC	MP15T
Production Dates	1974-02 to 1980-11	1975-08 to 1984-08	1984-10 to 1987-11
Total Built	246	255	42
Length	47'8"/48'8"	49'2"	50'2"
Engine	12-645E	12-645E	8-645E
Horsepower	1500	1500	1500
Alternator/Generator	D32U (Generator)	AR10 (Alternator)	AR10 (Alternator)
Traction Motors	D77B	D77B	D77B
Weight x 1000 lb	248	248	248

MP15DC
- Similar to SW1500, but 3 feet longer and with Blomberg trucks.
- Most have low-profile air-filter box ahead of cab.

MP15AC
- Dash 2 technology.
- No front-mounted radiator or intakes.
- Roof-mounted radiators and frame-level air intakes.
- Exhaust silencer mandatory in 1980.
- Blomberg trucks standard.

MP15T
- Single exhaust stack, indicating turbocharged 8-645E engine.
- Blower-duct bulge ahead of the cab, right side only.
- Central air-intake ahead of cab on left side.
- Radiator section similar to that of MP15AC.
- Headlight/numberboard box slightly larger than MP15AC.
- Blomberg trucks standard.

Developed to enhance the dual-service capabilities of EMD's heavy-duty switcher line, the MP15 superseded the SW1500 in February 1974. Just weeks after turning out Kentucky & Indiana Terminal 82 and 83, the last SW1500's built, La Grange outshopped the first MP15's —Missouri Pacific 1530-1534. At first glance, the MoPac MP15's appeared to be little more than beefed-up SW1500's on Blomberg trucks. However, the advances went beyond the obvious upgrade to road trucks. Lengthened by 3 feet over the SW1500, the MP15 could not only accommodate Blomberg trucks, but it could be ballasted to a heavier gross weight and carry a larger fuel tank, increasing maximum capacity from 1100 to 1400 gallons. Built-out sandboxes that had been optional on the SW1500 and were included on the NdeM SW1504's became standard, boosting the supply of sand from 30 to 50 cubic feet.

For the first few months of production, early MP15's, including

Milwaukee Road MP15AC's 453 and 474 mingle with other EMD's, including MILW SD40-2's and Amtrak F40PH 311, at Milwaukee, Wis., on April 18, 1982. The Tunnel Motor-style radiator section differentiates the MP15DC, while the dual exhaust stacks of the non-turbocharged 12-645 distinguish it from the MP15T.

P&LE 1574-1583 and Union R.R. 10-14, retained the overall similarity to the SW1500. However, the emergence of MoPac's second MP15 order brought a significant change in the appearance of the locomotive. Outshopped from La Grange in September 1974, MP 1535-1544 featured an air-filter box reminiscent of that found on the SW1504,

Long Island's 23 MP15AC's were purchased for dual service and employed in both freight and commuter service. On delivery from La Grange, Long Island MP15AC 167 rolls eastward in the consist of a Conrail freight on April 30, 1977.

although smaller and absent of louvers. This feature is found on many—but not all—subsequent MP15's.

Initially, the switcher models in EMD's catalog were passed over when La Grange unveiled the Dash 2 line of technologically revamped road locomotives in 1972. Three years later, Dash 2 technology finally trickled down to the lowly yard engine as EMD introduced the MP15AC.

Riding Blomberg trucks and measuring 49 feet, 2 inches between the pulling faces, the MP15AC— powered by the same 1500-h.p., 12-645E prime mover found in the MP15—packed a host of Dash 2 series enhancements, from a redesigned electrical control system with transistors, printed circuit boards and solid-state modular components replacing a maze of hard-wired circuitry, switches, contacts and relays, to an A.C. transmission, with an AR10/D14 alternator/rectifier replacing the D32 main generator used the MP15 and older models.

The most visible change, though, was in the cooling system, with the adoption of a radiator section and cooling system based on that of the SD40 and SD45T-2. Indeed, the new arrangement left the front of the MP15AC looking more like the rear of a "Tunnel Motor" SD than any EMD switcher. Appropriately enough, SP, the railroad that inspired development of the Tunnel Motor concept, was the first road to order MP15AC's, taking delivery of Nos. 2702-2731 in August and September 1975.

Sensitive to the fact that some customers might find the enhanced technology of the MP15AC unnecessary and unnecessarily expensive for a locomotive normally confined to the yard limits, EMD continued to catalog the original MP15, redesignating it as MP15DC for distinction. Sales for the two models ran neck and neck, with the MP15AC out-selling the D.C. version by only nine units.

Shortly after the last MP15AC rolled off the line at La Grange in August 1984, EMD released the latest, and last, version of the MP15, the turbocharged MP15T. The addition of a turbocharger allowed the MP15T's eight-cylinder 645E engine to produce the same 1500 horsepower as the earlier models with four fewer cylinders and the resultant savings in maintenance and fuel. The turbocharged 8-645E's single exhaust stack (versus two stacks for the normally aspirated 12-645E in other MP15's) and the blower-duct bulge ahead of the cab on the right side of the hood readily differentiate the

Just over a month old, Seaboard System MP15T 1208 works at Jacksonville, Fla., in December 1984. The single stack of the MP15T's turbocharged 8-645 engine, along with the right-side blower bulge and left-side central air intake, separate the MP15T from its normally aspirated MP15AC counterpart. Seaboard System purchased 41 of the 42 MP15T's built, with a single unit going to Dow Chemical in May 1987. *Mark R. Lynn*

MP15T from its kin. Seaboard System, now part of CSX, bought all but one of the 42 MP15T's built. In May 1987, nearly a year and a half after Seaboard's final MP15T's were delivered, EMD outshopped a single MP15T for Dow Chemical. Carrying road number 957, the lone unit quietly made history as the last EMD-built end-cab switcher.

The first GP15-1, Chicago & North Western 4400 was part of a 25-unit order delivered in June and July 1976. C&NW 4400-4424 were built with conventional air filters (as indicated by the rows of louvers behind the cab) rather than the inertial air filters that were standard on later GP15's. *Mark R. Lynn collection*

	GP15-1	GP15AC	GP15T
Production Dates	1976-06 to 1982-03	1982-11 to 1982-12	1982-10 to 1983-04
Total Built	310	30	28
Length	54'11"	54'11"	54'11"
Engine	12-645E	12-645E	8-645E3C
Horsepower	1500	1500	1500
Alternator/Generator	D32 (Generator)	AR10 (Alternator)	AR10 (Alternator)
Traction Motors	D77B	D77B	D77B
Weight x 1000 lb	240-261	261	240

GP15-1
- Tunnel Motor-style radiator section and cooling system with roof-mounted radiator and frame-level air intakes.
- Single radiator, vs two rads on GP15T.

GP15AC
- Externally identical to GP15-1.
- AR10 alternator instead of trade-in D32.
- Missouri Pacific 1715-1744 only units built.

GP15T
- Single exhaust, indicating turbocharged 8-645E3C engine.
- Twin radiators; larger radiator air-intake section.

Devised at the request of Chicago & North Western, the GP15 was designed to compete with the road's capital-rebuild program for aging GP7's and GP9's. Essentially a road-switcher version of the MP15, the GP15-1 comprised an unusual blend of new and old technology, from its Tunnel Motor-style radiator section and cooling system, to a bare-bones "Dash 1" electrical system designed to accommodate remanufactured components, particularly main generators, traction motors and trucks, from GP7 and GP9 trade-ins.

Reviving the concept of reusing components from trade-in locomotives, a practice that peaked in the mid-1960s as roads turned back first-generation diesels for credit toward new power, EMD endeavored to keep the GP15-1 pricetag as competitive as possible with the rebuild option. Nevertheless, many roads opted to rehab existing units, and sales of the baby Geep were decidedly lackluster. Many roads simply couldn't justify the purchase

Frisco's 25 GP15-1's were also built without inertial air filters, as shown by SL-SF 112 at Fort Smith, Ark., on December 30, 1977. *Mike Condren*

of new locomotives for low-priority yard, local and transfer service, where aging road units—rebuilt, or not— seemed to work just fine.

Fortunately for EMD, a few roads, four to be specific, did buy into the GP15-1 concept. Chicago & North Western and Frisco opted for 25 each when the model was introduced in

1976, while Conrail and Missouri Pacific fell for the baby Geep in a big way. With a single 1979 order, Conrail picked up 100 GP15-1's to replace a fleet of tired F's, Geeps and Alcos inherited from its bankrupt predecessors. MoPac, meanwhile, bought early and bought often, taking delivery of 60 GP15-1's in four separate orders in 1976, and 100 more by the spring of 1982. Released from La Grange in March 1982, MP 1705-1714 were the last GP15-1's built.

Holding title to more than half of the 310 GP15-1's produced, MoPac commissioned a variation on the theme with one final order for vest-pocket Geeps in late 1982. While the use of rebuilt, trade-in components—particularly the D.C. D32 main generator—was one of the cornerstones of the GP15 concept, MP specified new AR10 alternators in its last 30-unit order and the GP15AC was born.

Externally similar to its "Dash 1" forerunner, the GP15AC featured an A.C. transmission similar to that of state-of-the-art Dash 2 EMD's, rather than the D.C. drive comprised of first-generation trade-in components incorporated into the GP15-1. The design enhancement made the new model more compatible with contemporary power but generated no additional orders. MoPac 1715-1744 were the only GP15AC's built.

Even before Missouri Pacific's

Members of the largest GP15 fleet, Missouri Pacific 1609 and 1604 work back to back at Dolton, Ill., on April 19, 1986. Between 1976 and 1982, MoPac accumulated a fleet of 160 GP15-1's, along with 30 GP15AC's. Built with a new AR10 A.C. current alternator instead of a trade-in D32 D.C. current main generator, the GP15AC is externally identical to the GP15-1.

customized GP15AC's hit the road, EMD made a last-ditch effort to boost sales of the 15 Series with the introduction of the AR10-equipped GP15T. "T," in this case, stood for turbocharger, the addition of which allowed the GP15T to use a more fuel-efficient eight-cylinder 645E prime mover to produce the same 1500 horsepower as the normally aspirated 12-645E engine in the GP15-1 and GP15AC. The single

exhaust stack of the turbocharged engine, along with twin radiators and a larger radiator air-intake, make the GP15T easily distinguishable from its 15 Series companions.

Despite the improvements, the GP15T attracted only two customers. C&O took delivery of 25 dynamic brake-equipped GP15T's in the fall of 1982, while a trio for Florida's Apalachicola Northern closed out production of the model in April 1983.

Working Barr Yard in Riverdale, Ill., on September 11, 1985, dynamic-brake-equipped C&O GP15T 1512 represents the Cadillac of the vest-pocket Geeps, the GP15T. The single exhaust stack of the turbocharged 8-645E3C engine, along with twin radiators and a larger radiator air-intake section, differentiate the GP15T from its normally aspirated kin. The only GP15's built with dynamic brakes, C&O 1500-1524 account for all but three of the GP15T's built.

The last GP15T built, Apalachicola Northern 722 is one of three delivered to the Florida short line in April 1983. AN 720-722 were built without dynamic brakes and, in common with the very first GP15's, lack inertial air filters.
Bill Folsom, Mark R. Lynn collection

Working on BN at Aurora, Ill., on July 13, 1994, EMD BL20-2 121 represents a unique combination of old and new technology. EMD BL20-2 demonstrators 120-122 were built on the frames of ex-Burlington Northern GP9's and featured a turbocharged, rebuilt 16-567 engine mated with an AR10 alternator and Dash 2 electrical system. Outshopped from La Grange in mid-1992, the three demonstrators were the only BL20-2's built.

	BL20-2
Production Dates	1992-05 to 1992-08
Total Built	3
Length	56'2"
Engine	16-567
Horsepower	2000
Alternator	AR10
Traction Motors	D77
Weight x 1000 lb	250

BL20-2
- Built on GP7/GP9 frame.
- Carbody similar to GP39-2, but lacks inertial air filters.
- GP60M-style dynamic brake housing.
- EMD 120-122 only units built.

N early a decade after GP15 production ceased, EMD revived the "BL" series designation in another attempt to crack the rebuild market and compete with GE's Super 7 series. Built on the frames of a trio of ex-Burlington Northern GP9's of CB&Q, NP and SP&S heritage, BL20-2 demonstrators 120-122, outshopped from La Grange in mid-1992, bore no resemblance to the pre-Geep, BL1 and BL2 models of the late 1940s. Neither did they resemble GP9's, at least not from the frame up.

On the inside, the BL20-2 married the technology of two generations, with a rebuilt 16-567 engine (turbocharged to boost the output from 1750 to 2000 h.p.) mated to an AR10 alternator and Dash 2 electrical system. Although the GP9 frame,

The builder's plate on EMD BL20-2 121, one of the last locomotives outshopped from La Grange, is stamped "8-92."

trucks, traction motors, fans and prime mover were rebuilt and reused, the locomotive received an all-new cab and carbody, basically that of a standard second-generation Geep. Still, the BL20-2 has an unmistakable appearance, due to the absence of inertial air intakes behind the cab and the use of a squared-off dynamic brake assembly similar to that of a GP60M.

Competing in one of the toughest fields in the locomotive business, the three BL20-2 prototypes demonstrated for 2 years, but won no orders. Redeployed to EMD's lease fleet in 1994, they are now in the employ of Locomotive Leasing Partners, a joint venture by GATX Capital and EMD Leasing.

Blomberg trucks and a familiar-looking radiator section are the only hint that CIT Financial GP15D 1508, demonstrating on Pacific Harbor Lines at Wilmington, Calif., on August 17, 2001, is an EMD locomotive. Based on MotivePower's MP1500D, the 1500-h.p., Caterpillar-powered GP15D is built for EMD at MPI's Boise, Idaho, shop. CIT Financial's 10 CEFX-lettered lease units are the only GP15D's built so far. *David Lustig*

	GP15D	GP20D
Production Dates	2000-06 to current	2000-06 to current
Total Built	10	40
Length	56'2"	56'2"
Engine	12-170B15 (CAT 3512)	16-170B20 (CAT 3516)
Horsepower	1500	2000
Alternator	KATO 8P6.5-2250	KATO 8P6.5-2250
Traction Motors	D78B	D87B
Weight x 1000 lb	256	260

GP15D
- Externally similar to M-K MK1500D and MP1500D.
- High-profile cab; pug nose, low-profile hood.
- Single exhaust stack, two radiator fans.
- Blomberg trucks.

GP20D
- Externally similar to M-K MK1500D and MP2000D.
- High-profile cab; pug nose, low-profile hood.
- Single exhaust stack, two radiator fans.
- Optional dynamic brake.
- Blomberg trucks.

Electro-Motive's latest entries into the switcher/road-switcher market, the 1500-h.p. GP15D and companion 2000-h.p. GP20D are the products of a unique alliance involving EMD, Caterpillar Inc., and Motive Power Industries' Boise Locomotive. Although the model designations, minus the "D" suffix, of course, are familiar, the high-cabbed, pug-nosed GP15D and GP20D could never be confused with any of the locomotives built by La Grange or London. They *do*, however, bear a striking resemblance to MPI's MP1500D and MP2000D models, as well as the MK1500D of MPI predecessor MK Rail. And well they should, for the GP15D and GP20D are in fact refined versions of the Boise-design locomotives. Indeed, the EMD models are produced by the same Boise, Idaho, plant as their MPI forerunners under the terms of a purchase and supply agreement established between the EMD and MPI in 1998.

In common with Boise's MK/MP1500D and MP2000D, the GP15D and GP20D locomotives are powered by Caterpillar 3512 and 3516 series diesel engines, in an arrangement made possible by a related, but independent, deal struck between Electro-Motive and Caterpillar. The landmark agreement allows EMD to use CAT 3500 series engines and KATO traction alternators in locomotive applications worldwide. As such, the Caterpillar 3512 and 3516 diesels in the GP15D and GP20D carry EMD 170 series designations; the GP15D's 12-cylinder 3512B as GM12V170B15 and the GP20D's V-16 3516B as GM16V170B20.

While retaining many of the Boise design features, including the use of remanufactured Blomberg trucks and D78B traction motors, EMD brought a host of refinements and proprietary enhancements to the new line of Boise-built Geeps. At the top of the list is EMD's EM2000 Advanced Locomotive Computer, a microprocessor control system that monitors and manages everything

Equipped with an optional dynamic brake package and powered with a 2000-h.p. Caterpillar engine, CIT Financial GP20D 2008 works alongside GP15D 1508 on the PHL at Wilmington, Calif., on August 17, 2001. Like the GP15D, the GP20D is a Boise-built EMD model based on MotivePower's MP2000D. CIT Financial lease units CEFX 2001-2040 are thus far the only GP20D's built. *David Lustig*

from excitation and load control to engine management, adhesion control and onboard diagnostics.

Like their Boise Locomotive and M-K predecessors, the GP15D and GP20D have had limited success. As of this writing, only 50 units have been built: 10 GP15D's and 40 GP20D's, all for CIT Financial's locomotive lease fleet.

Viewed from overhead at Sayre, Pa., Lehigh Valley 313 reveals the main identifying features of the GP38-2, the dual exhaust stacks of a normally aspirated 16-645E3 engine and two radiator fans. The turbocharged GP39-2 has a single exhaust stack.

GP38-2
- Two exhaust stacks, indicating normally aspirated 16-645E3 engine.
- Two radiator fans.

DASH 2 FEATURES
(not on all orders)
- Right-side-only water-level sight-glass window.
- Battery box covers bolted, rather than hinged.

GP39-2
- Single exhaust, indicating turbocharged 12-645E3C engine.
- Two radiator fans.
- Last 20 built (MKT 360-379) in GP49 carbody.

DASH 2 FEATURES
(not on all orders)
- Right-side only water-level sight-glass window.
- Battery box covers bolted, rather than hinged.

	GP38-2	GP39-2
Production Dates	1972-01 to 1986-07	1974-08 to 1984-06
Total Built	2222	239
Length	59'2"	59'2"
Engine	16-645E3	12-645E3C
Horsepower	2000	2300
Alternator	AR10	AR10
Traction Motors	D77B	D77B
Weight x 1000 lb	245-281	250-277

When EMD unveiled its Dash 2 locomotive series in 1972, the differences between the old and new models were largely internal, the most significant change being the introduction of the Dash 2 line's solid-state, modular electrical control system. From beefed-up engine components to increased tractive effort and reduced exhaust emissions, EMD listed some 40 component changes and refinements in the Dash 2 locomotives, but in most instances the external changes were subtle. Such is the case with the GP38-2.

Like the GP38, the GP38-2 is easily differentiated from other models by the twin exhaust stacks of its non-turbocharged 16-645 series engine, and by the presence of two cooling fans above the radiator section at the rear of the hood.

Differentiating the GP38-2 from the GP38 is a more difficult task. Very early GP38-2's were built with the pre-Dash 2 radiator section used on GP38's. In mid-1972, EMD introduced a more compact radiator section.

Dash 2 details, including the right-side only, water-level sight-glass (in the hood door to the left of the word "Union") and a bolted, rather than hinged, battery box cover (front-right corner, ahead of the cab) are evident on Union Pacific GP38-2 2017 at Eastport, Idaho, on June 23, 1974.

The roof fans were moved noticeably closer together and a single-piece radiator grill replaced the two-piece arrangement on older units. By 1976, EMD began outfitting new units with a built-out corrugated radiator grille that gradually became standard on all new locomotives.

Other Dash 2 differences are subtle—and inconsistent. One of the most reliable features is the water-level sight-glass window cut into a

Mexico's Ferrocarril Chihuahua Al Pacifico and Nacionales de Mexico ordered GP38-2's with high short hoods and steam generators for passenger service. Built in the spring of 1982, NdeM 9901-9909 were the last North American locomotives built with steam generators. En route to Mexico after a financing-related delay, NdeM 9907 is at Decatur, Ill., on July 4, 1983. *Allen Rider, Mark R. Lynn collection*

The high short hoods on all 257 Southern Railway GP38-2's, including 5191, at St. Thomas, Ont., on November 22, 1987, are strictly cosmetic.

right-side hood door near the radiator section of most—but not all—Dash 2's. The new high-traction Blomberg-M truck, identified by the presence of damping struts and a steel-rubber composite in lieu of leaf-springs, was offered strictly as an option, and many GP38-2's, including hundreds riding on the trucks of traded-in Geeps and F-units, were delivered on conventional Blombergs. The change from a hinged and latched battery box access door to a bolted-on access plate identifies most Dash 2's, but BN specified the traditional hinged door on its GP38-2's. The presence of paper air filters, identified by the filter box located behind the central air intake, and available on both GP38's and GP38-2's, is not a distinguishing feature in itself. However, prompted by clearance problems encountered by Long Island GP38-2's delivered in January 1976, the contours of this box were altered on those and many subsequent units delivered to other roads. The revised box, with the upper edges beveled inward, is an aid in identifying later GP38-2's.

Picking up where the GP38 and GP38AC left off, the GP38-2 was a consistent best-seller. Between January 1972 and July 1986, La Grange and London turned out a total of 2222 GP38-2's for 59 customers in the United States, Canada and Mexico. Most were stock locomotives, with options limited to standard items such as dynamic brakes and Blomberg-M trucks. However, several hundred were built to custom specifications. MoPac's GP38-2's were outfitted with the road's unique four-stack exhaust, while Mexico's NdeM and CH-P commissioned 31 units (29 of which went to NdeM) with high short hoods and steam generators for passenger service. NdeM closed out the era of the dual-service Geep, taking delivery of 10 GP38-2's with steam generators tucked in their high short hoods. Completed at La Grange in June 1982, NdeM 9901-9909 were the last North American locomotives built with steam generators.

Canadian National specified its newly designed "comfort cab" on the final 51 of its 111 GP38-2's. Built in 1973, CN 5560-5610 were the first Geeps to be equipped with the new cab. Along with standard-cab sister 5505, CN 5573 rests on the shop track at Capreol, Ont., on February 22, 1975.

All 257 Southern Railway GP38-2's were built with high short hoods—not to accommodate steam generators, but in accordance with the road's unusual policy to shun low-nose locomotives. Forecasting the shape of things to come, CN commissioned custom-designed "comfort cabs" on the final 51 of its 111 GP38-2's.

A reliable, unglamorous work-horse, the GP38-2 stands as one of the most successful locomotives built. More than 15 years after London outshopped CP 3135, the last new GP38-2, more than 90 percent of the 2222 units built, many of them approaching 30 years of age, remain in service.

Eclipsed by the success of the

Two radiator fans and the single exhaust stack of the turbocharged 12-cylinder 645E3C engine identify the GP39-2, as illustrated in a broadside view of D&H 7603, at Buffalo, N.Y., on September 24, 1978.

GP38, the GP39, which had sold only 23 units during its entire run, was almost lost in the transition to the Dash 2 line. Indeed, the GP39-2 was suspiciously absent from EMD's initial Dash 2 catalog. Only after Santa Fe expressed interest in a turbocharged, medium-horsepower, four-axle road-switcher for work in high-altitude terrain did the GP39-2 rise from the ashes.

While Santa Fe opted for turbocharged power due to its ability to out-perform normally aspirated engines at high altitudes, a more significant advantage of the turbocharger is increased horsepower. As a result, the GP39-2 packs a 12-cylinder 645 series engine, which, by virtue of having a turbocharger, produces 300 more horsepower with four fewer power assemblies than the GP38-2's 16-cylinder 645. The 12-645E3 engine, with its single exhaust stack and unmistakable turbocharged whine, immediately separates the GP39-2 from its normally aspirated cousin, the GP38-2.

Santa Fe's interest and the advantages of turbocharging notwithstanding, the GP39-2 was still outsold by the GP38-2 at a ratio of nearly 10 to 1. Not surprisingly, Santa Fe amassed the largest GP39-2 fleet, purchasing a total of 106 units, albeit in five separate orders delivered over 6 years. Other GP39-2 owners included Burlington Northern, with 40, and D&H and Reading, who purchased 20 apiece. Kennecott Copper picked up 33 units, all but 4 of which were customized with high cabs and high under-clearance for use in its Utah open-pit mine operations. Phelps-Dodge, meanwhile, purchased a single GP39-2 for its New Cornelia branch out of Ajo, Ariz.

Kennecott Copper purchased 33 GP39-2's, all but four of which were customized with high cabs and high under-clearance for use in its Utah open-pit mine operations, as shown by KCC 794 at Copperton, Utah, on September 2, 1983. KCC 794 also features the built-out corrugated radiator grilles that became standard on all EMD's by the late '70s. *David R. Busse*

MKT 363, at St. Louis, Mo., on September 12, 1985, is not what it seems. The last GP39-2's built, MKT 360-379 were outshopped from La Grange in the spring of 1984 with standard GP39-2 machinery housed in the carbody of EMD's latest four-motor hood unit, the GP49.

While many observers presumed Phelps-Dodge 33, delivered in August 1981, was the last GP39-2, the model was in for one more revival—with a twist. In the spring of 1984, La Grange outshopped 20 MKT GP39-2's numbered 360-379. Mechanically, at least, the locomotives were GP39-2's; however, the machinery was housed in the carbody of EMD's latest four-motor hood unit, the GP49. Ironically, this was the carbody design that had debuted several years earlier with the release of a half-dozen prototype-demonstrators carrying model designation GP39X.

One of six GP39X testbeds, Southern 4602 carries white extra flags at Ludlow, Ky., on January 31, 1981. All six were built to Southern specs, with high short hoods and long-hood forward, and numbered SOU 4600-4605. Similar in appearance to the GP50, the 12-645-powered GP39X, a prototype-testbed for the GP49, has two radiator fans compared with three on the GP50. *Bryan Rice*

	GP39X	GP49
Production Dates	1980-11	1983-08 to 1985-05
Total Built	6	9
Length	59'2"	59'2"
Engine	12-645E	12-645F3B
Horsepower	2600	2800
Alternator	AR15	AR15
Traction Motors	D87	D87
Weight x 1000 lb	269	250

GP39X
- Similar to GP50, but with two radiator fans instead of three.
- Southern/NS 4600-4605 only examples of GP39X built.
- All built with high short hood, long-hood forward.

GP49
- Similar to GP39X, but all are low-nose.
- Two radiator fans.
- Alaska 2801-2809 only GP49's built.

Traditionally, EMD has employed the "X" suffix in model designations to indicate prototype locomotives. The GP39X is no exception. In November 1980, La Grange turned out six 2600-h.p., 12-645-powered GP39X locomotives as part of its program to develop the GP49, a 50 Series replacement for the GP39-2. Similar in appearance to the GP50, but with two radiator fans instead of three, the GP39X prototypes were built to Southern Railway specifications. Configured with high short hoods, set up for long-hood forward operation, painted and lettered Southern 4600-4605, the locomotives were, in fact, EMD-owned prototypes.

The GP49 was soon added to EMD's 50 Series lineup as a 2800-h.p. model and the Southern units were likewise upgraded. There was, however, very little interest in the new model. Southern did retain its

Beyond the low noses, L-shaped windshields, snow shields, hood-top snow baffles and winterization hatches over their forward radiator fans, Alaska GP49's 2801 and 2803, at Anchorage, Alaska, on August 14, 1994, are little different from the GP39X prototypes. Alaska 2801-2809 are the only GP49's built. *J. David Ingles*

GP39X prototypes, but ordered no GP49's. In fact, only the Alaska Railroad expressed serious interest in the GP49. ARR acquired the only nine units built; four in 1983 and five more in 1985.

A broadside view of C&O 4173 at Chatham, Ont., on October 18, 1973, illustrates the main identifying features of the GP40-2: the single exhaust stack of a turbocharged 16-645E3 engine and three radiator fans.

	GP40-2	GP40-2L	GP40P-2
Production Dates	1972-04 to 1986-11	1974-03 to 1976-05	1974-11
Total Built	903	233	3
Length	59′2″		62′8″
Engine	16-645E3	16-645E3	16-645E3
Horsepower	3000	3000	3000
Alternator	AR10	AR10	AR10
Traction Motors	D77B	D77B	D77B
Weight x 1000 lb	257-282	263	281

GP40-2
- Single exhaust, indicating turbocharged 16-645E3 engine.
- Three radiator fans.
- Right-side-only sight-glass window in hood on most Dash-2's.

GP40-2L
- CN-design comfort cab.
- Single exhaust, indicating turbocharged 16-645E3 engine.
- Three radiator fans.

DASH 2 FEATURES
- Right-side-only, water-level sight-glass window.
- Battery box covers bolted, rather than hinged.

Note: GO Transit 9808-9814, 707-710 and CN 9633-9667 are standard GP40-2's built with CN-design comfort cab. These units are not designated GP40-2L.

GP40P-2
- Single exhaust, indicating turbocharged 16-645E3 engine.
- Flared radiators with three radiator fans.
- Steam generator compartment behind radiators.
- SP 3197-3199 only units built.

Externally, the GP40 was barely affected by the transition to the Dash 2 line. Except for the small oblong-shaped water-level sight-glass window in a right-side hood door just below the radiators, the visible difference between a late GP40 and an early GP40-2 is barely perceptible. On the inside, though, it's a completely different story.

EMD incorporated a wealth of technological advances and mechanical improvements into the Dash 2 design. From the rails up, the new model line was enhanced with some 40 component changes and redesigns. The D77 traction motor and AR10 alternator were refined, and the 645 series engine was fortified with redesigned main, turbocharger and camshaft bearings, along with toughened pistons and chrome-plated stainless-steel piston rings. The greatest technological leap of all, though, was behind the electrical cabinet doors. Transistors, printed circuit boards and a control system featuring solid-state

Several railroads, Boston & Maine among them, purchased GP40-2's without dynamic brakes. Leading symbol freight NE-2, B&M "non d/b" GP40-2's 316, 310 and 314 approach East Deerfield, Mass., on March 2, 1978. Other roads that declined to order the dynamic brake option on their GP40-2's include DT&I, FEC, RF&P and CN.

modular components were the hallmarks of the radically redesigned Dash 2 electrical control system. The elaborate maze of hard-wired circuitry, ponderous relays, interlocks and bulky switches that defined the electrical systems of earlier locomotives was gone for good.

As far as the GP40-2 was concerned, one of the most significant Dash 2 improvements could

be found right where the wheels met the rail. Adhesion and wheel-slip control had been the GP40's Achilles heel since the model's introduction in 1966. Enhanced wheel-slip control, a key element of Dash 2 betterments, gave the GP40-2 a surer footing and gave its sales performance a shot in the arm.

From the Alaskan wilderness to the deserts of Mexico, the GP40-2

Although all 233 GP40-2L's built are outfitted with CN-design comfort cabs, the "L" in the model designation refers not to the cab, but to the model's lightweight frame. The design of this frame causes the GP40-2L to sit slightly higher than a standard GP40-2, as revealed in examination of CN GP40-2L 9412 and GP40-2 9636, rolling through Princeton, Ont., on October 7, 1992. Other than the slight difference in frame height, there is no visible distinction between the GP40-2L and the 46 standard GP40-2's built with comfort cabs: CN 9633-9667 and GO Transit 9808-9814, 707-710.

enjoyed modest acceptance, but sales were pushed over the top when two railroads fell for the 3000-h.p., four-motor hood in a big way. Chessie System, whose B&O, C&O and WM components purchased over 200 GP40's, continued its love affair with the Dash 2 version of the high-horsepower B-B, amassing a fleet of nearly 350 GP40-2's. Canadian National took the GP40-2 and made it its own.

Built with CN's own custom-designed "comfort," or "safety," cab, equipped with Positive Traction Control (PTC), a wheelslip control system developed in-house by the road's own technical research personnel, and constructed on specially designed lightweight frames, CN's GP40-2L's were distinctive, innovative and harbingers of the new face of dieseldom.

The so-called comfort cabs, which first appeared on CN M420's and GP38-2's built in mid-1973, were designed by the railroad in cooperation with running-trade representatives. Featuring increased collision protection as well as such crew amenities as refrigerators, hot plates and coffeepots, the cabs became a CN signature and were more or less unique to Canada for the next 15 years. Union Pacific picked up on the concept in 1989, ordering SD60M's and Dash 8-40CW's with a revised version of the "Canadian cab." Within a few years, the CN-inspired innovation became standard on almost all production locomotives and has become known as the "North American cab."

While the comfort cab was the most distinguishing feature of the

CN GP40-2L, the unique "L" model designation referred not to the cab but to the locomotive's lightweight frame. A custom design ordered by the railroad, the lightweight frame was devised to allow increased fuel and sand capacities without exceeding CN's gross weight and axle-loading standards. To achieve this, the GP40-2L frame employed steel I-beams with a taller but thinner web than normal. As a result, these locomotives sit slightly higher than a standard GP40-2.

Not all comfort-cab GP40-2's have the "L" designation. CN's final order, 35 units numbered 9633-9667, were built to standard GP40-2 specifications. As a result, they sit noticeably lower than their GP40-2L kin and have reduced fuel and sand capacities to compensate for the heavier frame. Essentially identical to CN 9633-9667, 11 GP40-2's were built for the Government of Ontario's Toronto-area commuter operator GO Transit. With the exception of GO 703, which went to Miami, Fla., commuter carrier Tri-Rail, the GO

Flared radiators, extra-length frames and a steam generator compartment behind the radiator section identify the passenger-equipped GP40P-2, which is essentially a Dash 2 version of the GP40P built for Central of New Jersey in 1968. Purchased for San Francisco Bay Area commuter service, SP 3197-3199 were the only GP40P-2's built. Far from Bay Area commutes, all three SP GP40P-2's work freight through Macdona, Texas, on February 25, 1986. The units were bumped permanently from passenger work by CalTrain F40PH-2's in the late '80s. *Mark R. Lynn*

GP40-2's were sold to CN when the Toronto commuter authority standardized its fleet with the F59PH.

GO Transit was not the only carrier to order GP40-2's customized for commuter duty. Searching for a

locomotive to replace F-M Train Masters in San Francisco Bay Area commute service, Southern Pacific commissioned a trio of steam-generator-equipped GP40P-2's. Similar to GP40P's built for CNJ in

1968, SP 3197-3199 were delivered in November 1974 with the same SD45-style flared radiators as their Jersey predecessors, but with reduced fuel and water capacities, extended-range dynamic brakes and cab air-conditioning. No additional units were built, and the delivery of CalTrain F40PH's ultimately bumped the trio to freight service, where they became SP 7600-7602.

While GO and SP opted for custom-ordered commuter versions of the GP40-2, Mexico's Chihuahua-Pacifico and Sonora-Baja California exercised a standard EMD option dating back to the days of the GP7 and requisitioned dual-service GP40-2's with steam generators in their high short hoods. CH-P's 4 and S-BC's 9 were the only high-nose GP40-2's built. Along with 25 stock models on CH-P and 7 more on S-BC, they were the only GP40-2's purchased by Mexican roads.

In a conspicuous circumstance that speaks as much to the fortunes of the 50 Series as it does of the enduring popularity of its predecessors,

The only high-nose GP40-2's built were 13 steam generator-equipped units purchased by Mexican roads, 4 by Chihuahua-Pacifico and 9 by Sonora-Baja California. Boiler-equipped CH-P GP40-2 1022 leads low-nosed sister 1010 at Cuauhtemoc, Chih., on March 14, 1980. *Bob Wilt, Keith E. Ardinger collection*

GP40-2 production continued long after the introduction of its supposed 50 Series replacement, the GP50. Indeed, La Grange outshopped the last GP40-2's, Florida East Coast 433 and 434, in December 1986—one year after completion of the last GP50.

Outshopped from La Grange in December 1986, one year after completion of the last GP50, Florida East Coast 433 and 434 were the last GP40-2's built. Little more than a month old, FEC GP40-2 434—last of them all—carries white extra flags at Riviera Beach, Fla., on January 28, 1987. *Michael Reid, Keith E. Ardinger collection*

Flared radiators are the hallmark of the 23 GP40X testbeds built in 1977-78 as forerunners of the 50 Series. Experimental HT-B high-adhesion trucks were employed beneath ten of the testbeds, UP 9000-9005 and SP 7200-7201 and 7230-7231, while Santa Fe 3800-3809 and high-nosed Southern 7000-7002 were built with Blomberg trucks. Sporting silvered HT-B trucks, Union Pacific GP40X 9002—fresh from La Grange—glistens in the sun on March 4, 1978. *Mark R. Lynn*

	GP40X	GP50
Production Dates	1977-12 to 1978-06	1980-05 to 1985-11
Total Built	23	278
Length	60'2"	60'2"
Engine	16-645F3	16-645F3B
Horsepower	3500	3500
Alternator	AR10	AR15
Traction Motors	D87X	D87
Weight x 1000 lb	274-278	260

GP40X
- Single exhaust, indicating turbocharged 16-645F3 engine.
- Flared radiators; three radiator fans.
- Southern 7000-7002 built with high short hood, long-hood forward.
- SP and UP units built with experimental HT-B high-adhesion trucks.

GP50
- Single exhaust, indicating turbocharged 16-645F engine.
- Larger radiator grille than GP40-2; three radiator fans.
- Southern 7003-7092 built with high short hood, long-hood forward.
- "Free-flow" blower duct on late-production ATSF and BN models.
- BN 3158-3162 built with extended crew cabs.

Pushing the technology envelope ever further, EMD unveiled the 3500-h.p., four-motor GP40X in December 1977. A prototype for the planned 50-Series replacement for the GP40-2, the GP40X boasted a new version of the 645 series prime mover (the 16-645F3), experimental high-adhesion HT-B trucks and a new Super Series wheel-slip detection and control system. In one of the most exhaustive test programs of recent times, EMD fielded a total of 23 GP40X prototypes over the next 6 months. Immediately recognizable by their flared SD45-style radiators, the EMD-owned units wore the colors of their host railroads and were equipped according to the specifications of those roads.

Union Pacific was the first to sign up for the GP40X and ultimately received a half-dozen of the prototypes, all of which rode on HT-B trucks. The only other GP40X's built with the new HT-B's were Southern Pacific's four, which were also delivered with the optional

Distinguishing the GP50 from the otherwise similar-looking GP40-2 are the noticeably larger radiators necessary to meet the cooling demands of the 3500-h.p., 16-645F engine. Chicago & North Western 5089 was delivered in July 1980 as part of the first GP50 order.

L-shaped windshield and experimental "elephant ear" shrouds over their radiator sections. A test application investigated as an alternative to the Tunnel Motor concept, the shrouds were temporary fixtures and were later removed from the locomotives. Santa Fe specified Blomberg-M trucks for its 10 GP40X's, as did Southern for its trio. In keeping with tradition, the Southern locomotives were also

built with high short hoods and set up for long-hood forward operation.

The GP50 made its debut in May 1980 with the delivery of the first of 50 units for Chicago & North Western. The flared radiators and high-adhesion trucks that had been hallmarks of the GP40X prototypes were not employed on production-model GP50's. Instead, the 50 Series Geeps rode on Blomberg-M trucks

Missouri Pacific's 30 GP50's were the only examples of the model built without dynamic brakes. Wearing UP colors, but MoPac lettering, GP50 3523 rests with SD40-2 6028 at Dolton, Ill., on July 12, 1986.

and were outfitted with traditional vertical radiators. Distinguishing it from otherwise similar-looking GP40-2, the radiators of the GP50 are noticeably larger (8 inches taller) in order to accommodate the cooling demands of the 3500-h.p., 16-645F engine.

Teething pains, particularly problems with the 3500-h.p. 645F, plagued the GP50 from the outset, and the model was cursed with lackluster sales for the entirety of its relatively short 5-year run. Not coincidentally, the GP40-2, a model that the GP50 was expected to

replace, remained in concurrent production as an alternative to the intended heir to the high-horsepower B-B throne.

Only two of the four railroads that tested the GP40X went on to purchase GP50's. Southern championed the model and quickly amassed what

Confirming the configuration of Southern's high-nose GP50's, a bell and air horns adorn the long-hood "front" of SOU 7086 at Oakwood Yard, in Melvindale, Mich., on July 27, 1987. With 90 high-nose units built between 1980 and 1981, Southern held title to the largest and most distinctive GP50 fleet. They were also Southern's last high-nose EMD's.

Burlington Northern 3158-3162, last of the road's 63 GP50's, were built with extended cabs to accommodate the crews of cabooseless trains. BN 3160, at Denver, Colo., on December 21, 1996, features the free-flow blower duct (just below the air intakes behind the cab) that became standard in the mid-1980s. Delivered in November 1985, the crew cab units were the last GP50's built. *Robert E. Lambrecht*

would be the largest fleet—90 high-nose versions acquired between August 1980 and June 1981. Santa Fe, meanwhile, purchased exactly half that many. Missouri Pacific's 30 GP50's were the only examples of the model built without dynamic brakes. Frisco ordered 10 GP50's, but the road was merged into Burlington Northern before La Grange could complete the order. Class engine 3100 was delivered in full Frisco paint, but the remainder were outshopped as BN locomotives. BN picked up 53 more GP50's in 1985, the last 5 of which were equipped with extended cabs to accommodate the entire crews of cabooseless trains. Made redundant by reductions in the number of crew members required on cabooseless trains, the crew cab concept did not catch on, and BN 3158-3162 were the only locomotives built with this feature. Outshopped from La Grange in November 1985, they were also the last GP50's built.

Still in EMD paint, but renumbered 4607 for new owner Norfolk Southern, former GP59 demonstrator EMD 9 exits the Ohio River bridge at Ludlow, Ky., with SD40 1604 and GP50 7061 and train No. 179 on April 8, 1988. The experimental smoothed lines and rounded leading edges of the cabs, noses and pilots of the three GP59 demonstrators were not repeated on production GP59's.

	GP59	GP60	GP60M	GP60B
Production Dates	1985-06 to 1989-12	1985-10 to 1994-02	1990-05 to 1990-09	1991-07 to 1991-09
Total Built	36	294	63	23
Length	59'9"	59'9"	59'9"	59'9"
Engine	12-710G3	16-710G3	16-710G3	16-710G3
Horsepower	3000	3800	3800	3800
Alternator	AR15	AR17	AR17	AR17
Traction Motors	D87B	D87B	D87B	D87B
Weight x 1000 lb	260	270	282	273

GP59
- Carbody similar to GP50.
- Six engine-hood doors for 12-710 engine, vs. eight for 16-710.
- Seven handrail stanchions along hood, vs ten on GP60.
- Demonstrators EMD 8-10 have leading edges of cab and nose rounded and GP50-style dynamic brake blisters.
- NS 4609-4641, only production units, have boxy, late 60 Series dynamic brake housing.

GP60
- Carbody similar to GP50.
- Redesigned, boxier dynamic brake blister on units built after July 1989.
- Demonstrators EMD 5-7 have leading edges of cab and nose rounded.

GP60M
- Wide-nose, North American cab.

GP60B
- Cabless booster unit.

Electro-Motive ushered its venerable GP line into dieseldom's third generation with the release of GP59 demonstrator-prototypes EMD 8, 9 and 10 in June 1985. La Grange gave its first 60 Series Geeps a new prime mover (the 12-710G) and a new look —softening the angular lines of the spartan cab and pointed nose in an experimental effort to reduce aerodynamic drag. While EMD made it clear that the aerodynamic styling of the prototypes was strictly experimental and would not be employed in production units, the most radical 60 Series advancements were on the inside.

Hidden behind the electrical cabinet doors on the rear wall of the cab, the GP59 concealed a trio of microprocessors that monitored and managed a host of engine, cooling system and control functions. A hallmark of the 60 Series and the defining detail of third-generation locomotives, on-board microprocessors replaced hundreds of wiring circuits, dozens of relays and all

Norfolk Southern purchased all three GP59 demonstrators as well as the only production-model GP59's. One of 33 GP59's built for NS, Operation Lifesaver-painted 4638 illustrates the model's overall similarity to the GP60. However, six engine-hood doors—indicative of a 12-cylinder engine—and seven handrail stanchions (versus ten on the GP60) identify NS 4638, at Kansas City, Mo., on April 19, 1999, as a GP59. *Mark R. Lynn*

but one module card in what many observers consider to be one of the most significant technological advances since the dawn of dieselization.

The vanguard of new-generation Geeps, the 3000-h.p. GP59 was the low-end of the 60 Series line and caught the fancy of just a single buyer: Norfolk Southern. NS purchased the 3 GP59 demonstrators in October 1986—numbering them 4606-4608, right behind its 6 GP39X prototypes— and followed up with a single order for 33 more 3 years later. NS 4609-4641 emerged from GMD London in November and December 1989, and were the only production GP59's built.

The only La Grange-built GP60's, demonstrators EMD 5-7 were outshopped in October 1985 with styling that softened the angular lines of the cab and nose in an experimental effort to reduce aerodynamic drag. The distinctive look was repeated on the GP59 demonstrators, but was not implemented on any production units. Outfitted with SP-style headlights, the three demos idle at the Indiana Harbor Belt yard in Blue Island, Ill., on September 19, 1987.

If the 12-cylinder, 3000-h.p. GP59 was the Chevy of 60 Series Geeps, the 16-cylinder, 3800-h.p. GP60 was the Cadillac. The most powerful Geep ever, the GP60 made its debut in October 1985 as La Grange dispatched demonstrator-prototypes EMD 5, 6 and 7 on a continent-wide barnstorming tour. Other than having an extra set of hood doors to access the larger 16-cylinder engine, the GP60 demos were similar in appearance to their GP59 counterparts—right down to the experimental rounding of the leading edges of their cabs and noses. However, unlike the plain Jane '59's, EMD 5-7 were decked out with just about every option La Grange could muster, from three different styles of fuel filler connections and an SP-style headlight package (featuring nose headlights, oscillating lights and a rotating rooftop beacon), to cab air-conditioning.

Two years after the prototypes hit the road, EMD had its first order for production-model GP60's. Not surprisingly, the model's first customer was Southern Pacific, on whose rails the demonstrators had spent much of their time. More remarkable was the fact that SP 9600-9619 were built at London, not La Grange. The move gave credence to rumors that EMD was on the verge of shifting all production from La Grange to London. In 1988, EMD formally confirmed the move, announcing that the GM Diesel Division plant in London, Ont., would be the company's main locomotive-building facility and that production at La Grange would cease by 1991. EMD GP60's 5, 6 and 7 were the last Geeps built at La Grange.

While the GP60 fared better in the marketplace than the GP59, sales of the 3800-h.p. B-B reflected changing trends in the industry. The all-purpose, four-motor road unit was falling from grace with the major railroads as heavier, faster trains (even in the intermodal trade) became the order of the day and six-axle power became the staple of mainline railroading from coast to coast. Sales figures for the 60 Series underscore the trend, with the SD60 outselling the GP60 at a rate better than 3 to 1.

Still, the GP60 did make some significant sales. Santa Fe purchased 126 GP60's in three different versions. After picking up 40 standard GP60's, Santa Fe commissioned 63 custom-designed "North American cab" GP60M's and 23 cabless GP60B's in 1990-91. Ordered for service on the road's hottest intermodal trains, Santa Fe GP60M's 100-162 were the first new units delivered in the revived "Super Fleet" Warbonnet

paint scheme and the only wide-nose GP60's built. Companions to the '60M's, GP60B's 325-347 were the only cabless 60 Series locomotives built and were the first Geep B's built since EMD delivered 40 GP30B's to Union Pacific in 1963. Norfolk Southern switched from GP59's to '60's with the purchase of 50 GP60's in 1991-92, while Rio Grande's first— and last—60 Series units were a trio of GP60's delivered in the spring of

1990. With the SP-Rio Grande merger in 1988, D&RGW 3154-3156 joined the ranks of the largest GP60 fleet. Southern Pacific, first to sample the model, stuck with it to the end, amassing a fleet of 195 GP60's, 95 of them lettered for subsidiary Cotton Belt. In February 1994, London closed the book on 45 years of EMD/GMD Geep production, outshopping SP 9794, the last GP60 and perhaps the last road-freight Geep ever.

The differences between 50 Series and 60 Series four-axle hoods are apparent as Santa Fe GP60 4002 and GP50 3830 work east of Needles, Calif., on April 2, 1996. The primary distinction between the two models is the boxy 60 Series dynamic brake blister seen on GP60 4002. However, Santa Fe 3830 is further differentiated by the presence of the pre-1985 blower bulge. Post-1985 GP50's have the same free-flow blower duct as the GP60.

Southern Pacific purchased the first, last and largest fleet of GP60's, acquiring 195 units between December 1987 and February 1994. Nearly half of the SP fleet was lettered for subsidiary Cotton Belt, but an even 100 were pure Southern Pacific. Just delivered from GMD, SP 9758 and 9757 bask in the sun at CP's Quebec St., roundhouse in London, Ont., on June 26, 1991.

Rio Grande's first—and last—60 Series units were GP60's 3154-3156, built to SP specs in May 1990. Almost ready to ship, Rio Grande 3155 and 3156 work out on GMD's London, Ont., test track on May 23, 1990.

Santa Fe followed its 40 standard-cab GP60's with an order for 63 custom-designed North American cab-equipped GP60M's. The first new units delivered in the road's revived "Super Fleet" Warbonnet paint scheme, and the only 60 Series B-B's built with North American cabs, Santa Fe GP60M's 100-162 were delivered between May and September 1990. Business cars in tow, Santa Fe 104 passes the passenger depot in Fullerton, Calif., on November 26, 1991. *David R. Busse*

One of 23 Santa Fe GP60B's built in the summer of 1991, AT&SF 329 awaits a westbound ride at CP's Quebec St. yard in London, Ont., on July 19, 1991. Taking advantage of the cableless configuration, the dynamic brake equipment on the GP60B was moved forward, and away from the prime mover. Santa Fe 325-347 are the only GP60B's.

A six-motor version of the GP38-2, the SD38-2 is readily identified by the twin exhaust stacks of its non-turbocharged 16-645 series prime mover and by the presence of two radiator fans. The oval water-level sight-glass and bolted battery-box covers confirm the Dash 2 pedigree of Bessemer & Lake Erie SD38-2 873, at Greenville, Pa., on April 25, 1989.

	SD38-2	SDL39
Production Dates	1972-11 to 1979-06	1969-03 to 1972-11
Total Built	83	10
Length	68'10"	55'2"
Engine	16-645E	12-645E
Horsepower	2000	2300
Alternator	AR10	AR10
Traction Motors	D77	D77
Weight x 1000 lb	368-391	255

SD38-2
- Two exhaust stacks, indicating normally aspirated 16-645E3 engine.
- Two radiator fans.

DASH 2 FEATURES
- Right-side-only water-level sight-glass window.
- Battery box covers bolted, rather than hinged.

SDL39
- Approximately 10 feet shorter than standard SD model.
- Single exhaust, indicating turbocharged 12-645E engine.
- Export-style truck frames.

In keeping with EMD practice and nomenclature, the SD38-2 is essentially a six-motor version of the GP38-2. In common with its B-B counterpart, the SD38-2 is readily identified by the twin exhaust stacks of its non-turbocharged 16-645 series prime mover, along with the presence of two cooling fans above the radiator section at the rear of the hood. Unlike its B-B catalog companion, however, the SD38-2 was not a big seller. Indeed, the model was in production for fewer than 7 years and sold only 83 units. The 2000-h.p. C-C was well suited for low-speed drag service, and that is precisely the duty for which most SD38-2's were purchased.

Not surprisingly, ore and coal haulers accounted for nearly two-thirds of SD38-2 production, with steel roads taking the lion's share. U.S. Steel's Chicagoland heavy-hauler Elgin, Joliet & Eastern assembled the largest SD38-2 fleet, with 14 units purchased in 1974-75, while Bessemer & Lake Erie finished a

A number of roads, including Chicago & Illinois Midland, ordered SD38-2's without dynamic brakes. Built in May 1974, C&IM 73 is at Springfield, Ill., on April 14, 1977.

close second, with 13. Sister Duluth, Missabe & Iron Range, purchased 5 SD38-2's, and a single unit, appropriately numbered USS 1, was built in December 1975 for U.S. Steel's remote Cumberland Mine operation in southwestern Pennsylvania. Back in the Iron Range, Reserve Mining bolstered its fleet of SD9's, SD18's and rare SD28's with 9 SD38-2's, while in the heartland, coal-hauling Chicago Illinois & Midland picked up a half-dozen SD38-2's to supplement its fleet of aging SD9's and SD18's. Further south, Yankeetown Dock acquired a trio of SD38-2's

Only four Class 1 roads, Chicago & North Western, Frisco, L&N and SP, purchased SD38-2's, all of them acquired for heavy yard and transfer work. Built without dynamic brakes, C&NW SD38-2's 6654 and 6655 drag a transfer cut out of Yard 9, part of North Western's suburban Chicago Proviso Yard complex, on April 18, 1986.

(including YDC 20-21, the first two built) for its coal line in southern Indiana.

For the most part, traditional short lines and regionals passed on the SD38-2, with only three—one in the United States, two in Canada—taking delivery of the 2000-h.p. C-C's.

McCloud River Railroad's trio of SD38's were joined by SD38-2 No. 39 in August of 1974; British Columbia Hydro received three EMD-built SD38-2's between 1972 and 1974, while a quartet of GMD-built units went to the Northern Alberta Railways the following year.

Outshopped from London in December 1975, NAR 401-404 were the only Canadian-built SD38-2's.

With the exception of a handful of units acquired for heavy switching, transfer and yard work, the SD38-2 was all but overlooked by Class 1 roads. Southern Pacific's 6 SD38-2's were acquired in the spring of 1973 for use at its newly built hump yard at West Colton, Calif., while Chicago & North Western's 10, delivered in January 1975, were assigned to the road's Proviso Yard in suburban Chicago. Also built in January 1975 and acquired for yard work, were Louisville & Nashville's five SD38-2's, numbered 4500-4504. Frisco's four, two equipped with extended-range dynamic brakes, for use on the downhill hump at Tulsa, Okla., and two Memphis-assigned units with no dynamic brakes, were delivered in June 1979—the last SD38-2's built.

After selling only 54 units, the SD39 was dropped from EMD's catalog and La Grange offered no Dash 2 equivalent of the 2300-h.p., six-axle model. However, production of the custom-designed SDL39 did extend into the Dash 2 era. Commissioned by the Milwaukee Road as a replacement for Alco RSC2's assigned to with restrictive axle-loading limits, the SDL39 was built on a short, 55-foot, 2-inch frame, powered by a turbocharged

Although EMD did not offer a Dash 2 version of the SD39, production of the custom-designed SDL39 did extend into the Dash 2 era. Commissioned by Milwaukee Road for service on branch lines with restrictive axle-loadings, only ten SDL39's were built. The first five, MILW 581-585, were delivered in the spring of 1969, while the second group, MILW 586-590, were built in November 1972. Still in original paint, but soon to become Wisconsin Central, Milwaukee 584 is at SOO's Shoreham shop in Minneapolis, Minn., on April 16, 1986.

12-645 engine and rode on customized export trucks. The 2300-h.p. C-C tipped the scales at just 250,000 pounds and managed a light-footed axle-loading of just 20.8 tons per axle. Only 10 of the unique units were built. The first order, MILW 581-585 were delivered in the spring of 1969, while the final five, MILW 586-590, were built in November 1972.

One of more than 800 Burlington Northern SD40-2's, two-month-old BN 6719 leads a runthrough coal train at Joliet, Ill., on April 10, 1977.

	SD40-2	SD40T-2	SD40-2SS	SD40-2F
Production Dates	1972-01 to 1986-02	1974-06 to 1980-07	1978-03 to 1980-11	1988-11
Total Built	3945	312	9	25
Length	68'10"	68'10"	68'10"	68'10"
Engine	16-645E3C	16-645E3C	16-645E3	16-645E3M
Horsepower	3000	3000	3000	3000
Alternator	AR10	AR10	AR16	AR10
Traction Motors	D77/78	D77	D77	D77
Weight x 1000 lb	368	388-410	392	389

SD40-2
- Single exhaust, indicating turbocharged 16-645E3 engine.
- Three radiator fans.

DASH 2 FEATURES
(not on all orders)
- Right-side-only water-level sight-glass window.
- Battery box covers bolted, rather than hinged.
- HT-C high-adhesion truck (Conrail units built with older style truck)
- N&W 1625-1635, Southern 3201-3328 high short hood, long-hood forward.
- CN 5241-5363 built with comfort cab.

SD40T-2
- Tunnel Motor radiator section.
- Roof-mounted radiators, frame-level air intakes.
- Two radiator-access doors vs. three on SD45T-2.

SD40-2SS
- BN 7049-7053, no major external difference from SD40-2.
- UP 3805-3808 larger radiators and slightly longer carbody than SD40-2, eight door panels below radiators, vs seven on SD40-2.

SD40-2F
- Full-cowl carbody with comfort cab.

Take a good thing and make it better. That was the mandate given La Grange engineers when Electro-Motive put its entire road locomotive line back on the drawing board to develop the Dash 2 model series in the early 1970s. Re-engineered from the rails up, the Dash 2 line incorporated some 40 component changes and improvements, most of which focused on increasing reliability, ease of maintenance and operating efficiency.

The newly developed high-adhesion HT-C truck, in combination with modular WS10 wheelslip controls, increased average all-weather dispatchable adhesion from 18 to 21 percent. The 645E3 engine was fortified with toughened pistons, chrome-plated stainless-steel piston rings, and engine, turbo and camshaft bearings were redesigned. Significant improvements were also made to the AR10 alternator and D77 traction motor, but the defining Dash 2 difference was the introduction of the solid-state, modular electrical control system.

The absence of dynamic brakes on SOO 6619 is conspicuous as the late-model SD40-2 leads a westbound freight up Orr's Lake Hill west of Galt, Ont., on May 22, 1995. Only SOO, Missouri Pacific and Rock Island purchased SD40-2's without dynamic brakes. Outshopped from La Grange in July 1984, SOO 6618-6623 were the last SD40-2's built for a U.S. road.

The Dash 2's revolutionary electrical control system heralded a major advance in locomotive technology. The intricate maze of hard-wired circuitry and cumbersome switches, contacts, interlocks and relays that been an integral element of diesel locomotives since the early first-generation diesel days was history. In its place, the Dash 2 boasted a radically redesigned electrical control system made up of transistors

137

High-nose Southern SD40-2 3245 and low-nose NS 6191, built for former high-hood advocate Norfolk & Western, stand at St. Thomas, Ont., on November 27, 1986. Southern specified high short hoods and long-hood forward configuration for all 128 of its SD40-2's, while N&W dropped the high-nose option after its first 28 SD40-2's.

and printed circuit boards managed by solid-state modular components governing everything from voltage regulation, battery charging and excitation, to throttle response, wheel-slip control, dynamic braking and even sanders.

The first Dash 2 of all, KCS SD40-2 637, was outshopped from La Grange in January 1972. Externally, the new Dash 2 wasn't all that different from its SD40 predecessor: there were subtle changes in the sheet-metal work on the cab roof and battery boxes, the addition of a water-level sight-glass window on a right-rear hood door, and the new HT-C trucks. Outwardly, the most dramatic change was a 3-foot increase in the length of the locomotive's frame. Necessary to accommodate the longer HT-C trucks, the added length gave the SD40-2 one of its most distinguishing features, a spacious platform behind the rear hood—the famous "back porch."

KCS 637 didn't raise many eyebrows when she emerged from La Grange, but the plain white SD40-2 was the start of something big. EMD engineers had indeed taken a good thing and made it better. From increased tractive effort and reduced emissions, to a 10 to 15 percent boost in reliability, the SD40-2 decisively outperformed the SD40—on the road and in the marketplace. Including custom-designed derivatives, SD40-2 sales totaled nearly 4300 units.

Southern Pacific commissioned the first—and most famous—SD40-2 variant, the SD40T-2 Tunnel Motor. The Tunnel Motor concept was developed for SP as a remedy for cooling problems encountered by locomotives operating at high altitudes and in the superheated, exhaust-filled air of tunnels and snowsheds. The locomotive's radiators were relocated to the top of the hood and air intakes positioned just above the frame where they could pull in cooler and cleaner air in tunnels. The design was first introduced on SD45T-2's built for SP in February 1972 and modified for the SD40T-2, 2 years later. SP purchased a total 239 40T's, and Rio Grande, impressed with the custom package, took 73 SD40T-2's of its own.

Asterisks in the annals of SD40-2 production are nine SD40-2SS testbeds built with EMD's Super Series wheel-slip control, along with a higher-capacity AR16 traction alternator and a larger turbocharger. Built in April and May 1978, BN 7049-7053 are indistinguishable from production SD40-2's. However, UP 3805-3808, delivered in November 1980, have a slightly longer carbody and noticeably larger radiators.

Customer-specified options, from items as simple as air horns, to elongated low noses (generally extended to accommodate radio and electronic equipment for remote-control

helper operation), individualized dozens of SD40-2 orders. Southern upheld its long-standing tradition, specifying high short hoods on its 128 SD40-2's, while N&W switched to low noses after ordering its first 28 SD40-2's with high short hoods.

Others roads, notably BCR, CP, KCS, SP and UP, ordered extended-length low noses. Canadian National's 123 SD40-2's were all delivered with the road's signature "comfort cab." Conrail, leery of problems that Amtrak was experiencing with a modified

All 123 of CN's SD40-2's were built with the road's custom-designed comfort cab. Although GMD gave the units no special model designation, some observers add a "W" (for "wide nose") to distinguish the units from standard-cab locomotives. Leading GTW GP38AC 6211, SD40 5913 and GP40-2 6416 at Bayview, Ont., on April 24, 1998, CN 5359 shows off the lines of the CN comfort cab, as well as the SD40-2's famed "front porch."

Two fan-access doors just below the radiators on Southern Pacific Tunnel Motor 8366, at Mojave, Calif., on March 23, 1978, identify the locomotive as an SD40T-2. By comparison, the SD45T-2 has three access doors in the same location. The optional extra-length nose, extended to accommodate radio and electronic equipment for remote-control helper operation, is available only on the SD40T-2 as the 20-cylinder SD45T-2's machinery occupies almost the entire frame.

version of the HT-C truck, ordered its SD40-2's with the older, pre-Dash 2 version of the Flexicoil-C truck.

EMD wrapped up SD40-2 production with the completion of NdeM 13001-13004 in February 1986. However, CP Rail, operator of the third-largest bought-new fleet of 40-2's, talked GM into building one final order of 3000-h.p., 645-powered C-C's. Not just any SD40-2's, mind you, but 25 cowl-carbodied SD40-2F's. Sporting comfort cabs, tapered cowl carbodies and console control stands, and equipped with Positive Traction Control, CP 9000-9024 were the only SD40-2F's built. Outshopped from GMD London in November 1988, they were the last of the SD40 line—the most successful model in Electro-Motive history.

Union Pacific 3275 and 3808 illustrate several SD40-2 variations, along with the difference between the SD40-2 and the SD40-2SS. Longer radiators and eight, rather than seven, hood doors beneath the radiators identify UP 3808 as an SD40-2SS testbed. Built in July 1974, UP 3275 has an optional 116-inch nose (compared to the 88-inch standard) and its radiator grilles are the original version, compared to the built-out, corrugated radiator grilles on the 3808, which was built in November 1980.

More than 2 years after La Grange built the last SD40-2's (NdeM 13001-13004 in February 1986), CP Rail took delivery of 25 custom-built, full-cowl SD40-2F's. Outshopped from GMD London in November 1988, CP 9000-9024 were the last of the SD40 line. CP SD40-2F 9017 dwarfs RS23 8029, making an odd couple on the shop track at St. Luc, Que., on October 20, 1990.

Assigned to the westbound *Chief*, Amtrak SDP40F's 527 and 508 depart Chicago for Los Angeles on April 15, 1977. Amtrak purchased 150 custom-designed, steam-generator-equipped SDP40F's between June 1973 and August 1974. The steam-generator stacks are evident behind the radiator fans of both units.

SDP40F
- Full-cowl carbody, similar to FP45, but lacking front stairwell and platform.
- HT-C trucks.

F40C
- Similar to SDP40F, but with corrugated body panels.

	SDP40F	F40C
Production Dates	1973-06 to 1974-08	1974-03 to 1974-05
Total Built	150	15
Length	72'4"	68'10"
Engine	16-645E3	16-645E3
Horsepower	3000	3200
Alternator	AR10	AR10
Traction Motors	D77/78	D77/78
Weight x 1000 lb	396-400	364

Although the SD40-2 was designed and marketed as a heavy-duty freight locomotive, two agencies ordered customized versions for passenger service. Searching for a suitable replacement for aging E-units inherited with the takeover of the nation's inter-city passenger service, Amtrak commissioned the SDP40F. The 396,000-lb., full-cowl, steam generator-equipped SDP40F bore a strong outward resemblance to the FP45, but on the inside, its machinery and electrical systems were essentially that of an SD40-2.

Between June 1973 and August 1974, Amtrak took delivery of 150 SDP40F's, but their reign as the nation's premier passenger power would be short. Derailments, several at high speed, cast a shadow on the locomotive's reputation. By early 1977, the SDP40F had been involved in more than a dozen derailments, and the locomotive's modified "hollow bolster" version of the HT-C truck was being investigated as a contributing factor.

Surrounded by the locomotives it was designed to replace, Amtrak SDP40F 600 mingles with E8's and E9's at Central Terminal in Buffalo, N.Y., on April 30, 1977. While the first 40 SDP40F's, Amtrak 500-539, featured a pointed nose similar to that found on earlier EMD F45's and FP45's, the remainder were built with flattened noses, as seen on No. 600.

As Amtrak, EMD, the AAR and FRA launched in-depth investigations and exhaustive tests of the locomotive and its tracking characteristics, the SDP40F gained dubious distinction as "the most tested locomotive in history." The derailments were eventually attributed to the lateral forces developed by water (for the units' steam generators) sloshing in the on-board tanks. EMD devised a fix for the problem, but the controversy had shaken Amtrak's faith in the locomotives. The cost of upcoming overhauls and conversion to HEP soon sealed the fate of the nearly

The F40C is basically an SDP40F with an HEP generator instead of steam generators. However, corrugated stainless-steel carbody panels give the slightly shorter F40C an entirely different look. Working home turf, North West Suburban Mass Transit F40C 45 wheels bilevels past Milwaukee Road's Tower B12 in Franklin Park, Ill., on April 17, 1977.

new SDP40's. In 1977, at age 3, 40 Amtrak SDP40F's were traded in to EMD on a like number of F40PH's, which were built using the engines, alternators, traction motors and other parts of the ill-fated SDP's. By 1988, all but 18 of the 150 SDP40F's built had been traded-in on Amtrak F40's. EMD retained 4 of the trade-ins for use as testbeds, but the rest were stripped of reusable components and scrapped.

The 18 Amtrak SDP40F's that were not traded in were dealt to Santa Fe in September 1984 in an exchange that saw the passenger carrier pick up 25 AT&SF CF7's and 18 SSB1200's in return for the SDP's. Santa Fe reconditioned and modified the former passenger haulers for freight service and reclassified them as SDF40-2's.

But for some stainless-steel carbody panels and a few feet of length, the F40C is essentially an SDP40F with an HEP alternator in lieu of steam generators. A commuter-hauling cousin to the SDP40F, the F40C's 16-645E engine was boosted to 3200-h.p. to help compensate for the load drawn by the 500-kw alternator used to supply head-end power for train lighting, heating and air-conditioning. While the HEP equipment could demand up to 700 h.p., its compactness allowed the F40C to be built on the standard SD40-2 frame, rather than the longer FP45 framed needed by the steam generator-equipped SDP40F. As a result, the F40C was not afflicted with any of the tracking or ride-quality afflictions that plagued its SDP40F brethren.

While most Amtrak SDP40F's were returned to EMD as F40PH trade ins, 18 were dealt to Santa Fe in exchange for 25 AT&SF CF7's and 18 SSB1200 switchers in September 1984. The units were overhauled and modified for freight service at Santa Fe's San Bernardino, Calif., shops and redesignated "SDF40-2's" by the railroad. Fresh from San Bernardino, Santa Fe 5251 (formerly Amtrak 511) leads No. 188 over Cajon Pass on February 10, 1985. The train's consist includes two more ex-Amtrak SDP40F's, along with a GP50 and an SD45-2. *David R. Busse*

Custom designed for commuter service on the Milwaukee Road lines out of Chicago, a total of 15 F40C's were constructed in the spring of 1974, just months after Amtrak began taking delivery of SDP40F's. The first 13 units were financed under the auspices of, and lettered for, the North West Suburban Mass Transit District, while the remaining 2 were lettered for the North Suburban Mass Transit District. The only F40C's built, all 15 are now in the employ of Chicagoland commuter authority Metra, but the unique units have spent their entire lives on Milwaukee Road turf, working commuter trains between Elgin, Fox Lake and Chicago.

Although lacking the signature flared radiators of its SD45 predecessor, the SD45-2 retains a distinctive look, with radiators significantly larger than those of the SD40-2, topped by three widely spaced radiator fans. The 20-cylinder locomotive's machinery fills the frame, thus eliminating the expansive end-platforms found on the SD40-2, as seen on Erie Lackawanna SD45-2 3675, at Binghamton, N.Y., on September 25, 1975. EL's 13 SD45-2's were built with oversize 5000-gallon fuel tanks, forcing the main air-reservoirs and aftercooler piping to be relocated to the rear of the long hood, where their presence is indicated by two rows of louvers, unique to the EL units.

	SD45-2	SD45T-2
Production Dates	1972-05 to 1974-09	1972-02 to 1975-06
Total Built	136	249
Length	70'8"	70'8"
Engine	20-645E3	20-645E3
Horsepower	3600	3600
Alternator	AR10	AR10
Traction Motors	D77B	D77B
Weight x 1000 lb	386-391	410

SD45-2
- Radiator section significantly longer than SD40-2.
- Three radiator fans—spaced further apart than on SD40-2.
- Locomotive occupies more of frame—no expansive end platforms.

SD45T-2
- Tunnel Motor radiator section.
- Roof-mounted radiators, frame-level air intakes.
- Three radiator-access doors vs. two on SD40T-2.

As a rule, the outward appearance of most EMD models was little changed with the introduction of the Dash 2 line. The SD45, however, is a notable exception. The flared radiators that had been the hallmark of the SD45 were eliminated, and replaced by conventional vertically mounted rads on the SD45-2.

The flares may be gone, but radiators remain an identifying feature of the SD45-2. To satisfy the cooling demands of the locomotive's 20-cylinder 645 series prime mover, the radiators of the SD45-2 are significantly longer and the cooling fans atop the rads are spaced further apart than those of the SD40-2.

While the SD40-2 machinery fits comfortably on its standard 68-foot, 10-inch frame, the SD45-2, with its carbody elongated to accommodate the larger radiators as well as the 20-645 engine, is a tight fit, even on the longer 70-foot, 8-inch frame. The famed front and back "porches" that characterize the SD40-2 are nowhere to be found on its 3600-

On March 19, 1978, Santa Fe SD45-2's 5661 and 5668, along with F45 5901 and SD26 4654, lead a westbound manifest past the ruins of Tunnel 4 east of Bealville, Calif.

h.p. big brother, the SD45-2.

Before the introduction of the Dash 2 line, crankshaft and main bearing failures in older SD45's, coupled with the 20-645's appetite for fuel and its higher maintenance costs, took a toll on sales of the

3600-h.p. muscle machine. Although it had outsold the SD40 during the late '60s, the SD45 soon fell behind and its total pre-Dash 2 production of 1260 units fell shy of the 1285 SD40's sold to some 30 railroads from Labrador to Mexico.

One of eight Santa Fe SD45-2's converted to cabless boosters, AT&SF 5517 (built as No. 5700 in 1973) illustrates the relocation of dynamic brake equipment to the area formerly occupied by the cab, as well as the widely spaced radiator fans common to all SD45-2's.

By the time EMD unveiled the SD45-2, La Grange had dealt with many of the SD45 maintenance issues and remedied the crankshaft and bearing problems that had afflicted the 20-cylinder 645 engine. However, the SD45-2 was no match for the runaway success of the SD40-2. Only Clinchfield, Erie Lackawanna, Santa Fe and Seaboard Coast Line stepped up to purchase stock-model SD45-2's, and just 136 units were built—a mere fraction of the nearly 4000 SD40-2's sold.

Long before the first stock SD45-2's were built, in fact, even before the Dash 2 line was officially launched, diehard SD45 advocate Southern Pacific commissioned EMD to build a custom version of the 3600-h.p. freighter. SP asked for a robust mountain goat of a locomotive that could perform in high altitudes and endure the superheated,

asphyxiating environment of tunnels and snowsheds. What it got was the SD45-2 Tunnel Motor.

The Tunnel Motor package gave the locomotive's rear section an unmistakable boxy look, with radiators repositioned to the top of the hood and air intakes located just above the frame where they could draw the coolest, cleanest available air in tunnels.

Among the earliest Dash 2's built, the SP SD45T-2's began rolling out of La Grange in February 1972. No other railroads signed up for the SD45T-2, but by June 1975, SP had amassed a fleet of 247 units, 166 of which carried subsidiary SSW reporting marks and Cotton Belt lettering.

Not to be confused with the SD45T-2 is the model's little brother, the 3000-h.p. SD40T-2. Also developed at SP's request, the SD40T-2 is, as the designation suggests, an SD40-2 customized with the Tunnel Motor package.

Similar at a glance, the two models can be distinguished by the three radiator-fan access doors above the rear air-intakes on the SD45T-2, compared to just two on the SD40T-2. Furthermore, the SD45T-2's elongated carbody fills the frame more than the SD40T-2.

A victim of rising fuel costs and the phenomenal success of the SD40-2, the SD45-2 ceased production after a run of less than three and a half years. The SD40-2 was clearly the standard freight locomotive of its time, while the '45, railroading's '60s-style muscle machine, had had its day.

The SD45T-2 is easily distinguished from its SD40T-2 counterpart by the presence of three fan-access doors just below the radiators, as seen on SP 9358 at Mojave, Calif., on March 30, 1999. The SD40T-2 has just two access doors in the same location. Further differentiating the two models is the fact that the SD45T-2 lacks the large end-platforms found on the SD40T-2.

Sporting a full headlight package, SP SD45T-2 9248 pauses with '60s-vintage muscle machines, SD45 8997 and U33C 8683, at Mojave, Calif., on March 23, 1978.

A 50 Series testbed, the SD40X marked the disappearance of the dynamic brake blister, a fixture on most EMD hood units since the days of the GP7. Relocated from the traditional location atop the prime mover, the dynamic brake equipment on the SD40X is positioned immediately behind the cab, as indicated by the grille behind the cab windows on KCS 700, at Heavener, Okla., on October 16, 1982. Built on a standard 68-foot, 10-inch SD40-2 frame, the SD40X is noticeably shorter than the production model SD50. *Paul Strang, Mark R. Lynn collection*

	SD40X	SD50S	SD50	SD50F
Production Dates	1979-09*	1980-12	1984-11 to 1985-05	1985-04 to 1987-07
Total Built	4	6	421	60
Length	68′10″	68′10″	71′2″	71′2″
Engine	16-645F3	16-645F3	16-645F3B	16-645F3B
Horsepower	3500	3500	3500-3600	3600
Alternator	AR16	AR16	AR16 (3500) AR11 (3600)	AR11
Traction Motors	D87Y	D87	D87Y (3500) D87A (3600)	D87
Weight x 1000 lb	387-393	390	368-394	390

SD40X
- SD50-style carbody on SD40-2 frame.
- Dynamic brake located between cab and central air-intake. No blister.
- KCS 700-703 only units built.

SD50S
- Nearly identical to SD40X.
- N&W 6500-6505 only units built.

SD50
- Frame lengthened to 71 feet, 2 inches.
- Dynamic brake located between cab and central air-intake. No blister.
- Six door panels below radiator grilles, vs eight in SD60.

SD50F
- CN-design comfort cab, full-cowl carbody.
- CN 5400-5459 only units built.

Following the GP40X prototypes of 1977-78, EMD broadened its program to advance beyond the successful Dash 2 series models with the construction of a quartet of 3500-h.p., six-motor "SD40X" testbeds. Built on standard SD40-2 frames and powered by the new 16-cylinder 645F3 prime mover, the four units began testing at La Grange in the summer of 1978 and were delivered as KCS 700-703 in September 1979.

From exhaust silencers and Q series, "quiet" radiator fans, to Super Series adhesion control system and improvements in the electrical system, the SD40X premiered a number of innovations and technological advances. The most noticeable external change was the relocation of the dynamic brake resistors from their usual position above the prime mover to cooler, cleaner space just behind the cab. The familiar dynamic brake "blister," a fixture on EMD hoods since the GP7, was nowhere to be found on the SD40X. Instead, the d/b equipment was housed in a 6-foot-

The first SD50's, Norfolk & Western 6500-6505, were delivered in December 1980. As indicated by N&W 6501, at Roanoke, Va., on November 7, 1981, the N&W units are nearly identical to the four KCS SD40X prototypes. The only SD50's built on the shorter SD40-2 frame, N&W 6500-6505 were redesignated "SD50S" when EMD adopted the 71-foot, 2-inch frame as the 50 Series standard. *Allen Rider, Mark R. Lynn collection*

long hood section inserted just between the cab and the central air intake. This reconfiguration simplified removal of the prime mover, put the dynamic brake in a more hospitable environment, and pushed the carbody

length to all that the 68-foot, 10-inch frame could accommodate.

KCS 700-703 were the second group of locomotives to carry the SD40X designation, which had previously been given to nine SD40

A few feet longer than, but otherwise similar to its SD40X roster mates, KCS 704, seen at Kansas City, Mo., on December 15, 1999, is the first production SD50 and one of ten on KCS. *Mark R. Lynn*

prototype-demonstrators built in 1964-65. While the '60s version of the SD40X lead to the most successful EMD model of all time, the second group of testbeds to carry the SD40X label were harbingers of EMD's first high-adhesion locomotive, the SD50.

The first SD50's, Norfolk & Western 6500-6506, were delivered in December 1980. Essentially identical to the four SD40X prototypes on KCS, they were the only SD50's built on the Dash 2-era 68-foot, 10-inch frame, which was overcrowded with the 50 Series machinery layout. Following the construction of the N&W units, EMD extended the length of its standard six-axle platform to 71 feet, 2 inches and all production SD50's were built on this frame. To differentiate the shorter preproduction units from their standard-length kin, the six N&W units were redesignated SD50S.

Kansas City Southern followed up its 1979 acquisition of the SD40X testbeds with the purchase of the first production SD50's, 10 units delivered in the spring of 1981. But for the elongated frame, KCS 704-713 were little different from their SD40X and SD50S forerunners.

Railroads were not beating down EMD's door to get SD50's. Many roads were reluctant to embrace the new model, preferring to stick with the tried and true SD40-2 instead. Yes, the SD50 was a child of the recession, but the 18-month gap between the delivery of the first and second production orders was due to more than just slow times.

EMD's decision to squeeze the 645 engine for all it was worth and power the SD50 with a 16-cylinder 645F rated at 3500, and later 3600 h.p., was greeted with skepticism in the offices of more than a few chief mechanical officers. Their concern was not unwarranted. Demanding from the 16-645F engine the same horsepower that had necessitated 20 cylinders with the E Series 645 would ultimately exact a costly toll.

Infirmities notwithstanding, the SD50's fortunes took a turn for the better by 1983, as orders began to trickle in. Over the next 3 years, CSX components B&O, C&O and Seaboard System took a total of 144 units and Conrail signed up for 135—all but the last 30 on pre-Dash 2 Flexicoil trucks. In the summer of 1984, Norfolk Southern received 20 SD50's set up to operate long-hood forward, while Rio Grande picked up 17 conventionally configured units.

Vanguards of a new generation, two units from the second Seaboard System order, SBD 8525 and 8526, were built in March 1984 with microprocessor controls. Carrying their SBD road numbers, but dressed in unlettered Seaboard gray, the two units were retained by EMD and employed to test microprocessor

In late 1984, EMD beefed up the SD50, boosting its horsepower rating from 3500 to 3600 and furnishing the model with an uprated alternator and traction motors. Despite the improvements, EMD made no change in the model designation, and, as shown by 3600-h.p. SD50 C&O 8567, there were no significant external changes to the model.

control systems developed for the 60 Series locomotive line. After several months of testing, the units were lettered and delivered to Seaboard System, but the writing was on the wall for the 50 Series. EMD had already added the 60 Series models to its catalog.

In late 1984, EMD boosted the SD50 from 3500 to 3600 h.p., an

The external differences between the SD50 and SD60 are subtle, almost imperceptible. However, close examination of C&NW SD50 7007 and SD60 8018, at Clinton, Iowa, with GP50 5055 on January 25, 1987, reveals the only major outward distinction between the two models. The SD50 is fitted with six door panels below the radiator grilles, compared to eight on the SD60.

increase that was not significant enough to warrant any change in the model designation, but included some notable component changes, including the switch from the AR16 alternator to the AR11 and equipping the units with 1205-amp D87A traction motors instead of the 1170-amp D87Y motors supplied with earlier units. Delivered in November and December 1984, Missouri Pacific 5000-5059 were the first uprated SD50's. During the final 14 months of SD50 production, Chicago & North Western, Conrail, C&O and Seaboard System all took delivery of units rated at 3600 h.p.

North of the border, Canadian National was the sole SD50 customer. However, CN ordered its own custom-designed, cowl-carbodied version designated SD50F. The London-built, 3600-h.p. SD50F incorporated several notable features of CN design, including the road's trademark comfort cab, a console control stand and the innovative "Draper taper." The brainchild of CN Assistant Chief of Motive Power William L. Draper, the so-called taper was a notch cut

The sole 50 Series customer north of the border, Canadian National took delivery of 60 customized, cowl-carbodied, 3600-h.p. SD50F's between April 1985 and July 1987. Factory fresh, with barely a trace of road dust, CN SD50F 5421 idles in the company of elderly RS18 3123 at MacMillan Yard, in Toronto, Ont., on September 28, 1985.

into the cowl carbody just behind the cab so as to afford the crew at least a limited line of sight to the rear without opening the cab-side windows. CN acquired a total of 60 SD50F's built between April 1985 and July 1987.

A transitional model, the SD50 overlapped the final years of SD40-2 production and the early years of the SD60. Its 16-645 pushed to the limit, the SD50 was plagued by engine failures and low reliability early in its service life. EMD sought to remedy the problems with factory rebuilds and warranty work, while some roads derated the troublesome locomotives. Mergers have folded most of the original SD50 production into the fleets of CSX, NS and UP, and all three roads have begun disposing of many of their SD50's upon expiration of their operating lease.

Assigned to a work train at East Logan, Wyo., on March 30, 1997, EMD-painted, Oakway SD60's 9034 and 9061 illustrate the model's outward similarity to the SD50. The external difference between the two models is limited to the number of hood doors below the radiator grilles: eight on the SD60, six on the SD50. However, the similarity is strictly cosmetic. The 710-powered, microprocessor-managed SD60 marked EMD's entry to dieseldom's third generation.

	SD60	SD60F	SD60M	SD60I
Production Dates	1984-05 to 1991-05	1985-09 to 1989-11	1989-01 to 1993-06	1993-04 to 1995-09
Total Built	537	64	461	81
Length	71'2"	71'2"	71'2"	71'2"
Engine	16-710G	16-710G	16-710G	16-710G
Horsepower	3800	3800	3800	3800
Alternator	AR11	AR11	AR11	AR11
Traction Motors	D87B	D87B	D87B	D87B
Weight x 1000 lb	368	387-395	395	395

SD60
- Nearly identical to SD50.
- Eight door panels below radiator grilles, vs six in SD50.

SD60F
- Externally identical to SD50F.
- CN 9900-9903, 5504-5563 only units built.

SD60M
- Wide-nose North American cab on otherwise similar SD60 carbody.
- Production units built 1989-91 have three-piece windshield.
- Production units built 1991-93 have two-piece windshield, tapered nose.

SD60I
- Isolated WhisperCab version of North American cab, identified by seam separating nose and cab components.

The SD60, save for a few extra hood doors beneath its radiators, is externally identical to the SD50. However, the similarities end there. The introduction of the SD60 in the spring of 1984 marked the arrival of not just a new model, but a new generation of EMD locomotives—the 60 Series.

Incorporating a new prime mover, the 710 series engine, along with a radically redesigned control system managed by a trio of microprocessors, the SD60 ushered EMD locomotives into the third generation.

The first SD60's, a quartet of blue and white prototype-demonstrators numbered EMD 1 through 4, were released from La Grange between May and July 1984. Another four testbeds, EMD-owned but painted as Norfolk Southern 6550-6553, emerged from La Grange in December 1984. Shortly thereafter, NS placed the first order for 60 Series locomotives—50 SD60's, which EMD began delivering in mid-1985.

In September 1985, GMD London

Standing on the wye behind the GMD plant in London, Ont., SOO SD60 6052 poses for the company photographer on October 25, 1989.

constructed four SD60 testbeds of its own. Externally identical to the CN SD50F's and painted as CN 9900-9903, the cowl-carbodied testbeds carried builder's plates bearing model designation SD50AF. Nevertheless, they were all 60 Series on the inside. After testing for several years, the units were sold to CN and are now considered SD60F's.

In the late 1980s, an industry-wide drive to improve the safety and comfort of locomotive cabs led both builders to develop their own production versions of the CN-designed, wide-nose "safety cab," or "comfort cab," which had been a standard feature on CN power since the M420's, GP38-2's and GP40-2L's of 1973-74.

Making their first revenue run, CN 9900 and 9901 lead M420 2568 and SD40 5225 through Paris, Ont., with train 410 on January 7, 1986. Completed at London in September 1985, cowl-carbodied testbeds CN 9900-9903 were among the earliest 60 Series units built. Their builder's plates are stamped SD50AF, but the 710-powered units are considered to be SD60's. In addition to the four prototypes, CN purchased 60 full-cowl, production model SD60F's in 1989. The only SD60F's built, the units are externally identical to the SD50F.

In January 1989, the first EMD model with the new wide-nose "North American cab," made its appearance when London out-shopped UP SD60M 6085, the first of a 25-unit order. Technically, the M stood for modified and designated the use of the North American cab. However, the new cab quickly became the standard. Several roads, notably CSX, Kansas City Southern and NS, resisted the change and continued to specify conventional cabs on their SD60's, but the die was cast and the face of the American freight locomotive was changing for good.

In 1993, EMD took the new cab design a step further, introducing the "WhisperCab," an isolated version of its North American cab. Unlike conventional locomotive cabs, the new cab was not welded in position, but floated on the underframe structure of the locomotive on a cushion of rubber mounts in an effort to increase crew comfort and reduce noise and vibration. Units equipped with the WhisperCab option have an "I" (for isolated cab) suffix added to their model designation. The first unit built with an iso-lated cab was Conrail SD60I 5544, outshopped from London in April 1993. Conrail purchased a total of 81 SD60I's, the only isolated-cab SD60's built.

More than just the cabs of the Conrail SD60I's were trendsetting. La Grange was no longer building locomotives, and London had more orders than it could handle, so 45 of the 81 units were assembled and painted under contract by the road's Juniata Shops in Altoona, Pa. Locomotive sales continued to boom through the 1990s, and assembly of new EMD locomotives by contract shops became commonplace.

Meanwhile, Canadian National, the road that started it all, continued to chart its own course in locomotive design. After purchasing 60 custom-tailored cowl-carbodied SD50F's and testing the "SD50AF" prototypes, CN ordered SD60's in the same cowl carbody. Designated SD60F, this custom version was sold only to CN, who purchased 60 new units along with the four testbeds.

The SD60 also lead the way in one of the most revolutionary programs at La Grange since the FT. A.C. traction prototypes for EMD's A.C. program, four SD60MAC testbeds were built in 1991-92, two at La Grange and two at London. These locomotives are covered in the section dealing with EMD A.C. traction models.

The first locomotive with EMD's new wide-nose "North American cab," UP SD60M 6085 rests beside the CP Quebec St. roundhouse in London, Ont., on delivery day, January 10, 1989. The three-piece windshield and original cab design lasted for just 2 years, being replaced in 1991 by a redesigned cab, with a two-piece windshield and tapered nose. UP 6085-6268, BN 9200-9249 and SOO 6058-6062 were built with the original cab and three-piece windshield.

EMD's redesigned North American cab was introduced in the winter of 1991 with the delivery of Burlington Northern's second 50-unit SD60M order. The two-piece windshield, and reshaped nose that tapers inward from the frame are illustrated by BN SD60M 9272, east of Hodge, Calif., on March 29, 1999.

Continuing to improve its cab design, EMD unveiled the WhisperCab on Conrail SD60I ("I" for "isolated" cab) 5544 in April 1993. Designed to improve crew comfort and reduce noise and vibration, the WhisperCab rides on a cushion of rubber mounts that isolate it from the underframe structure of the locomotive. The WhisperCab has become a common feature on EMD locomotives, but Conrail's 81 SD60I's were the only isolated-cab SD60's built. Conrail's Juniata, Pa., shops assembled and painted 45 of the road's 81 SD60I's, including 5641, leading GP40 3308 on the BUPI at Youngstown, Ohio, on August 30, 1995. As seen on CR 5641, a seam separating the nose and cab components identifies units built with the WhisperCab option.

Norfolk Southern, Illinois Central and Conrail (under NS direction) ordered conventional cab SD70's, even though the model was introduced with the North American cab-equipped SD70M as the standard. Unique to the conventional cab SD70 is the bulge on the right side of the nose, as seen on NS 2514 at Harborcreek, Pa., on August 26, 1996. This feature is necessary to accommodate Integrated Cab Electronics equipment within the smaller confines of the conventional nose. All SD70's ride on EMD's HTCR-II radial truck.

	SD70	SD70I	SD70M
Production Dates	1993-04 to current	1995-07 to current	1992-07 to current
Total Built	120	26	1063
Length	72'4"	72'4"	72'4"
Engine	16-710G3B	16-710G3B	16-710G3B
Horsepower	4000	4000	4000
Alternator	AR20	AR20	AR20
Traction Motors	D90TR	D90TR	D90TR
Weight x 1000 lb	394	398	390

SD70
- HTCR-II radial trucks.
- Bulge on right side of nose to accommodate Integrated Cab Electronics equipment.
- Large air-intake screen, below left-side radiators, for rear traction motor blower.

SD70M
- HTCR-II radial trucks.
- North American cab.
- Large air-intake screen, below left-side radiators, for rear traction motor blower.
- Flared radiator, split cooling version introduced on testbeds December 2000. Standard on production models as of 2002-01.

SD70I
- HTCR-II radial trucks.
- Isolated WhisperCab version of North American cab, identified by seam separating nose and cab components.
- Large air-intake screen, below left-side radiators, for rear traction motor blower.

An overhead view of CN SD70I 5613 and Dash 9-44CW 2545 at St. Paul, Minn., on August 1, 1998, offers a good overall comparison of contemporary EMD and GE locomotives, as well as an illustration of the distinct separation of the cab and nose sections of the isolated WhisperCab. Delivered between July and November 1995, CN 5600-5625 are the only WhisperCab-equipped SD70I's built to date.

An evolutionary progression from the SD60, the SD70 established a modest but meaningful increase in horsepower from 3800 to 4000. However, the model's most significant advancement was below the frame. The SD70 was the first production model to feature EMD's patented HTCR steerable radial truck. Electro-Motive's interest in radial-truck design dated to the early 1980s and included application of an experimental two-axle version on a Santa Fe GP50 in 1984 and the three-axle version on SD60 demonstrator EMD 3 in 1987. Development of the radial truck was a linchpin in EMD's A.C. traction program, and the first production HTCR trucks appeared on the SD60MAC prototypes of 1991-92. Nevertheless, the SD70 was the first model in the EMD catalogue with the high-adhesion radial truck.

Sporting the now-standard North American cab, riding on HTCR radial trucks and dressed in EMD maroon, silver and black, a trio of SD70M demonstrators numbered 7000-7002 introduced the new 70 Series model in the summer of 1992. The units' silvered HTCR trucks, the only major external difference between the SD70M's and their SD60M fore-runners, delineated far more than just a simple spotting difference. The radial truck stands as a revolutionary advancement in locomotive suspension, adhesion, ride quality and component life.

Once again, Norfolk Southern was first in line for the new model. However, NS, forward-thinking in some ways, ultraconservative in others, wanted nothing to do with the new North American cab. Instead, NS specified SD70's with conventional cabs and took delivery of 56 units in 1993-94. Purchasing its first new locomotives in years, Illinois Central also opted for the SD70 with a conventional cab, taking 40 units in two orders built in 1995

Standard equipment on all SD70's, the HTCR-II radial trucks on the SD70M immediately differentiate it from the similar-looking SD60M. Close examination of SD70M's SP 9809 and EMD 7011, grinding around Tehachapi Loop along with UP SD40-2 3949 on March 29, 1999, reveals additional distinctions. Minor changes introduced with the SD70 include three built-out hood doors just below the forward radiator section, along with the recessed hand-brake wheel located a few feet from the rear of the hood.

and 1999. Conrail, an early convert to the North American cab, reverted to conventional cabs for its last new locomotive order, 24 SD70's ordered by NS in anticipation of the Conrail breakup. In full Conrail dress, but built to NS specifications and carrying NS road numbers, CR SD70's 2557-

2580 were assembled in the road's Juniata shop in Altoona, Pa., during the latter half of 1998. These units were, of course, included in the NS share of Conrail assets when NS and CSXT divided Big Blue between them on June 1, 1999.

In contrast to NS and IC, Canadian National went to the other extreme, ordering EMD's top-of-the-line WhisperCab for its SD70's. Sharing the shop floor at London with IC's standard-cab SD70's in the second half of 1995, CN's 26 SD70I's are the only examples of the model built with the isolated-cab feature to date.

Somewhat of a sleeper in the EMD catalog, the SD70/SD70M sold just 209 units in its first 8 years of production, while sales of its A.C. traction counterpart, the SD70MAC, were comparatively brisk. In addition to the three demonstrator units and 22 EMD lease-fleet units, the only other SD70M's on the road by 1999 were 25 SP's built in 1994 and a trio built for the New York Susquehanna & Western in 1995. However, the model's sleeper status came to an

Dressed in EMD colors, lease-fleet SD70M's 7019 and 7011 lead SP SD45-rebuild 8671 through Canyon, Calif., on Cajon Pass, on November 16, 1996. Solid-maroon 7019 exhibits two left-side only changes introduced with the SD70. The blower bulge, just below the air intakes behind the cab, has been reconfigured to a smaller, rectangular outcropping, compared to the large, angled protrusion found on the SD60 and earlier models. At the rear of the hood, an extra grille—an air intake for the rear traction motor blower—has been added below the radiator grilles. These features are also present on the SD75I and SD75M.

abrupt end in October 1999, when UP ordered 1000 SD70M's for delivery over a three-to-four-year period.

The largest single-model locomotive order ever placed in North America, production of the 1000 UP SD70M's is being handled primarily by GMD-London and Bombardier's contract shop in Concarril, Cuidad Sahagun, Mexico. However, 46 units, UP 4119-4164, were built at Super Steel Schenectady, Inc., in Glenville, N.Y., and painted by Alstom at Hornell, N.Y.

Prototype-testbeds for modifications to bring new locomotives into compliance with EPA Tier 1 emission standards, UP SD70M's 4635-4639 emerged from London in December 2000. As part of modifications made to meet regulations set to take effect in 2002, the locomotives were outfitted with beefed-up radiators and a new cooling system, divided into independently controlled sections; engine jacket water is handled by one part of the radiators, water for the after coolers is managed by another. The newly engineered "split" cooling system was state of the art, but the demands of the split design made larger radiator cores a necessity, and the resultant flared radiators gave the units a look reminiscent of the SD45.

In 1999, Union Pacific ordered 1000 SD70M's, the largest single-model locomotive order ever placed in North America. Scheduled to be complete by 2004, production of the 1000 units has been handled primarily by EMD-London and Bombardier's contract shop in Concarril, Ciudad Sahagun, Mexico. However, 46 units, UP 4119-4164, were built at Super Steel Schenectady, Inc., in Glenville, N.Y., and painted by Alstom at Hornell, N.Y. London-built UP 4605 and 4606 wait outside CP's Quebec St. roundhouse on March 24, 2001. *William D. Miller*

Testbeds for modifications necessary to comply with EPA Tier 1 emissions standards, UP SD70M's 4635-4639 emerged from London in December 2000 with a new split cooling system and flared radiators reminiscent of the SD45. Engaged in preproduction testing, flared prototype UP 4635 rests at Neff Yard in Kansas City, Mo., on April 9, 2001.
Robert E. Lambrecht

EMD began outshopping production model Tier 1-compliant UP SD70M's with split cooling and flared radiators in January 2002. Just delivered, UP 4717 and 4720 bask in the sun at CP's Quebec St. roundhouse in London, Ont., on January 8, 2002.

BNSF SD75M 8252, leading Dash 9-44CW 659 and Dash 8-40CW 836 east of Needles, Calif., on April 2, 1996, reveals the only significant external difference between the SD75M and the SD70M, as well as their respective isolated cab counterparts. The beveled outcropping, visible beneath the inertial air-intake on the 8252, is present only on the SD75M and SD75I. Santa Fe 200-250 and Burlington Northern Santa Fe 8251-8275 are the only SD75M's built.

	SD75M	SD75I
Production Dates	1995-03 to current	1996-05 to current
Total Built	76	207
Length	72'4"	72'4"
Engine	16-710G3	16-710G3C
Horsepower	4300	4300
Alternator	AR20	AR20
Traction Motors	D90TR	D90TR
Weight x 1000 lb	394	394

SD75M
- HTCR-II radial trucks.
- North American cab.
- Similar to SD70M, with added bulge below inertial air-intake on right side.

SD75I
- HTCR-II radial trucks.
- Isolated WhisperCab version of North American cab, identified by seam separating nose and cab components.
- Similar to SD70I, with added bulge below inertial air-intake on right side.

R esponding to the 4400-h.p. rating of the popular GE Dash 9-44CW, EMD bumped the output of the 16-710G3 engine from 4000 to 4300 h.p., and the SD75 was born. Santa Fe, its successor Burlington Northern Santa Fe, CN and Ontario Northland have thus far been the only takers for the SD75M or the WhisperCab-equipped SD75I. EMD's most powerful D.C. traction freight locomotive, the SD75 bears a very close resemblance to its SD70 siblings. In fact, the beveled outcropping on the right side of the hood, just below the inertial air filters on the SD75M/SD75I, is the only major external difference between the two models.

Santa Fe/BNSF received the only SD75M's. Delivered between March and August 1995, the first SD75M's, Santa Fe 200-250, were also the last new locomotives delivered in the road's classic Warbonnet paint. The next 25 units, built between December 1995 and March 1996, also came in Warbonnet dress, but had BNSF initials emblazoned on

The isolated cab, identified by the seam separating the nose and cab components of the locomotive, is the only difference between the WhisperCab-equipped SD75I and the SD75M. One of the road's 175 SD75I's, CN 5755 works west of Paris, Ont., with Dash 9-44CW 2567 on December 14, 1998. The only other SD75I's are BNSF 8276-8301 and Ontario Northland 2100-2105.

their silver hoods and carried post-merger road numbers 8251-8275.

Beyond its isolated cab, the SD75I is otherwise similar to the SD75M. While neither version of the 4300-h.p., D.C. freighter has sold particularly well, sales figures for the SD75I are better than double those of the SD75M, thanks to Canadian National. While BNSF complemented its SD75M

fleet with 26 SD75I's, CN picked up a total of 175 units in three orders built between 1997 and 1999. The last 35 CN SD75I's were assembled in 1999 at Alstom's Montreal facility in the former CN Pointe St. Charles shops. At the same time, Ontario Northland, the only other SD75I customer, took 6 Alstom-assembled units built to CN specifications.

The appearance of the SD60MAC testbeds, as illustrated by BN 9500 at Murray Yard, in North Kansas City, Mo., on June 10, 1995, is similar to that of the SD60M. However, the SD60MAC rides HTCR-II radial trucks, and sports air intakes for the A.C. traction equipment at both ends of the long hood. Found on both sides of the locomotive, these vents are located just behind the cab, below the dynamic brake grille, and below the radiators near the rear of the hood. The only SD60MAC's built, EMD-owned, BN-painted 9500-9503 were returned to the builder in June 1998. *Robert E. Lambrecht*

	SD60MAC	SD70MAC
Production Dates	19910-06 to 1992-09	1993-11 to current
Total Built	4	1007
Length	74'0"	74'0"
Engine	16-710G3A	16-710G3C-ES
Horsepower	3800	4000
Alternator	TA17/CA7A	TA17/CA7A
Traction Motors	1TB2630	1TB2630
Weight x 1000 lb	390	415

SD60MAC
• HTCR-II radial trucks.
• North American cab with three-piece windshield.
• Air intakes for A.C. traction equipment on both sides of hood: below dynamic brake grille and below radiators.

SD70MAC
• HTCR-II radial trucks.
• North American cab with two-piece windshield.
• Air intakes for A.C. traction equipment in both sides of hood: below dynamic brake grille and below radiators.
• WhisperCab version of North American cab standard after 1995.

One of the most important technological advances since the development of the diesel-electric locomotive, A.C. traction, specifically, the use of alternating-current traction motors, has revolutionized heavy-haul railroading in the past decade. Traditionally, North American locomotives have been built with direct-current, D.C., traction motors since the dawn of the diesel. EMD changed all that in 1991.

While some railroads and builders (CP, for instance, who outfitted MLW M640 4744 with four Brown Boveri A.C. traction motors in 1984) dabbled with experiments in A.C. traction, it was EMD who took the concept and ran with it. In June 1991, EMD La Grange outshopped the first all-new heavy-haul North American A.C. locomotives, a pair of SD60MAC prototypes. A pair of London-built SD60MAC's joined the program in September 1992, and the quartet, painted as BN 9500-9503, soon hit the road for in-service testing. By the end of the decade, North

On the outside, the first 173 A.C. traction SD70MAC's built are almost identical to their D.C. counterpart, the SD70M. In fact, four small air-intakes for the A.C. traction equipment of the SD70MAC are the only discernable difference. As seen on BN 9438, at Fort Worth, Texas, on October 31, 1994, the vents—found on both sides of the locomotive—are located just below the dynamic brakes at the cab end of the hood, and immediately below the radiators near the rear of the hood. In March 1995, beginning with BN 9572, the isolated cab became a standard feature on the SD70MAC. BN 9400-9571 are the only SD70MAC's built without isolated cabs. *Mark R. Lynn*

American railroads had purchased over 3000 high-horsepower A.C. locomotives.

Custom-built on a 74-foot frame and riding on EMD's new HTCR radial truck, the SD60MAC was an amalgam of the SD60M and the fruits of more than a decade of A.C. traction research, development and

testing done by EMD and its A.C. partner, Siemens AG of Germany. Test units, including an ex-Amtrak SDP40F converted to EMD "Research vehicle" 268 outfitted with Seimens A.C. equipment and North America's first new A.C. locomotives, a pair of F69PHAC testbeds, paved the way for the SD60MAC, arguably the most

Although the isolated cab became standard on the SD70MAC in March 1995, EMD made no change in the model designation. Near Shawnee Jct., Wyo., on June 10, 1998, BNSF SD70MAC 9850 illustrates the WhisperCab-equipped SD70MAC, which, but for the extra air-intakes for the A.C. equipment, is externally similar to the SD70I.

innovative locomotive to roll out of La Grange since the FT's of 1939.

On the road, the SD60MAC demonstrators quickly established that A.C. traction was all that its proponents promised—and that the marriage of the alternating-current traction motor and EMD's steerable HTCR radial truck was a match made in heaven. The units made good EMD's promise that three MAC's could replace five SD40-2's in heavy-haul coal service, and the HTCR truck proved to be as revolutionary as the A.C. motors slung on its axles.

On the merits of the demonstrators' performance, Burlington Northern bought in. But not for SD60MAC's. In an unprecedented move, BN inked a $675 million order for 350 4000 h.p. A.C. drive SD70MAC's—sight unseen. Heralds of the new age, BN/EMD 9500-9503 would be the only SD60MAC's built. However, their offspring would number in the thousands. The A.C. revolution was underway.

A direct descendant of the SD60MAC, EMD's—and North America's—first production, heavy-duty A.C. locomotive was the SD70MAC. Basically an SD70M with A.C. drive, the SD70MAC was similar in appearance to its D.C. drive cousin. The '70MAC's extra 2 feet in overall length is barely discernable, and but for a pair of small, vented carbody openings on each side, one below the dynamic brake grille, the other below the rear radiator, the A.C. and D.C. versions of the SD70M are difficult to tell apart from the outside.

On the inside, it's another matter. Although the two models share everything from radial trucks to 4000-h.p. 16-710G3 prime movers and EM2000 microprocessors, behind the electrical cabinet doors, the SD70MAC is an entirely different beast.

The electrical system of any A.C. locomotive is even more complex than that of a conventional D.C. traction diesel-electric locomotive. In both cases, the locomotive's main alternator, or traction alternator, produces A.C. current, which is delivered to rectifiers and converted to DC power. In non-A.C. locomotives, this current is routed directly to the traction motors. In A.C. locomotives, the D.C. power from the rectifiers is delivered to banks of inverters, whose GTO's (Gated Turn On devices) "chop" the D.C. power to effectively produce the three-phase A.C. power, which is fed to the traction motors.

EMD A.C. locomotives employ one inverter bank per truck, in comparison to the GE design, which uses one inverter bank per traction motor. As a result, EMD A.C.'s must have an entire truck cut out in order to isolate a problem traction motor, while it is possible to cut out individual traction motors on GE A.C. locomotives.

A.C. traction motors are simpler, more reliable, more efficient and more durable than conventional D.C. traction motors, but their greatest attribute is adhesion. The maximum adhesion that a D.C. SD70M can achieve on dry rail is about 30 percent. By comparison, the SD70MAC boasts an average adhesion of 35 percent. All of this comes at a cost, though. A.C. traction can add between $500,000 and $1 million to the pricetag of a new locomotive, a fact that has helped a number of

In addition to BN and BNSF, four other roads have purchased SD70MAC's: Alaska (16), Conrail (15), CSXT (75) and TFM (75). Conrail SD70MAC's 4130-4144 were built to CSXT specs at CR's Juniata, Pa., shops and assigned to CSXT when the road was divided up with Norfolk Southern in June 1999. Still in full Conrail paint, CSXT-numbered, SD70MAC 785 rolls into Seneca Yard in Lackawanna, N.Y., on May 15, 2000.

roads make the decision to stick with D.C. traction.

Nevertheless, the SD70MAC quickly established itself as EMD's A.C. standard. BN's landmark 350-unit order became the foundation of a BN/BNSF SD70MAC fleet that now numbers more than 800 units that reign supreme over the road's Powder River Basin coal traffic.

While BN/BNSF purchases account for the lion's share of SD70MAC production, other roads, from Alaska

to Mexico, have picked up EMD's 4000-h.p., A.C. freighter. CSX, with a total of 90 SD70MAC's—including 15 Juniata-built, ex-Conrail units—holds title to the second-largest fleet. South of the border, Kansas City Southern's Mexican subsidiary Transportacion Ferroviaria Mexicana (TFM) has 75 Mexican assembled SD70MAC's, while in the extreme north, the Alaska Railroad has taken delivery of 16 70MAC's, one London-built and 15 assembled at Juniata.

The SD80MAC, with its redesigned carbody featuring a squared engine hood, oversize radiators and a separate dynamic brake compartment at the rear of its hood, is externally identical to the SD90MAC, which was unveiled just 3 months later. One of two demonstrators built in July 1995, EMD 8000 poses at CP Quebec St. in London, Ont., on July 14, 1995.
David T. Stowe

	SD80MAC
Production Dates	1995-07 to 1996-05
Total Built	30
Length	80′2″
Engine	20-710G3B-ES
Horsepower	5000
Alternator	TA22/CA8
Traction Motors	1TB2830
Weight x 1000 lb	420

SD80MAC
- HTCR-II radial trucks.
- Oversize, flared radiators.
- Squared engine hood.
- Dynamic brake equipment located in hood section behind radiators.
- Isolated WhisperCab version of North American cab, identified by seam separating nose and cab components.

The advent of A.C. traction and the resultant increase in available adhesion and starting tractive effort touched off a new horsepower race as both builders sought to take advantage of the untapped potential of A.C. systems capable of handling more horsepower than existing locomotives could deliver. EMD revived the 20-cylinder engine and took the lead in 1995 with the introduction of the 5000-h.p. SD80MAC. Riding radial trucks and built on a new 80-foot, 2-inch frame, with an isolated cab, oversize radiators, a reconfigured machinery layout (with dynamic brake equipment located at the very rear of the hood) and a 20-710G3 under its redesigned hood, the SD80MAC was the big kid on the block.

London outshopped SD80MAC demonstrators 8000-8001 in July 1995, followed by 28 Conrail units delivered between November 1995 and May 1996. Chicago & North Western's planned 15-unit SD80MAC order fell victim to the UP merger in

Conrail purchased all 30 SD80MAC's built, including EMD 8000-8001, which became Conrail 4128-4129 at the close of their demonstration tour. Renumbered for new owner CSXT, but still in Conrail paint, SD80MAC 803, built as CR 4108, leads former demonstrator 4128 at Cheektowaga, N.Y., on August 9, 1999.

1995. No other roads expressed interest in the 20-cylinder, 5000-h.p. A.C.'s, and Conrail added the demonstrators to its fleet at the end of their tour, giving Big Blue all 30 SD80MAC's built.

Designed to be upgraded to 6000 h.p. upon perfection of the 265H engine, the SD90MAC is outwardly identical to the SD80MAC, although the '90 convertible is powered by a 4300-h.p., 16-710 engine instead of the 20-cylinder 710 in the SD80MAC. As with all EMD A.C. traction locomotives, the WhisperCab is standard. Wearing the short-lived "We Will Deliver" scheme, UP SD90MAC 8039 works through St. Paul, Minn., on July 31, 1998. The unit's single exhaust and squared hood confirm that a 710, rather than a 265H engine is under the hood.

	SD90MAC	SD90MAC-H	SD90MAC-H 11	SD89MAC
Production Dates	1995-10 to current	1996-08 to 1999-01	1998-06 to current	2000-06 (testbed)
Total Built	410	22	46	1
Length	80'2"	80'2"	80'2"	80'2"
Engine	16-710G3-ES	GM16V265H	GM16V265H	GM12V265H
Horsepower	4300	6000	6000	4500
Alternator	TA22/CA8	TA22/CA8	TA22/CA8	NOT AVAILABLE
Traction Motors	1TB2830	1TB2830	1TB2830	1TB2830
Weight x 1000 lb	415	420	425	NOT AVAILABLE

SD90MAC
- Upgradable 710-engine version externally identical to SD80MAC.
- HTCR-II radial trucks.
- Oversize, flared radiators.
- Squared engine hood.
- Dynamic brake equipment located in hood section behind radiators.
- Isolated WhisperCab version of North American cab, identified by seam separating nose and cab components.

SD90MAC-H
- Dual exhaust stacks, beveled engine hood indicating twin-turbo 265H engine. Otherwise identical to upgradable SD90MAC.

SD90MAC-H II
- Cab and nose reprofiled to accommodate rectangular windows and full-height front door.
- Number of radiator fans reduced from three to two.
- Rear of hood reprofiled to smoother design.
- Dual exhaust stacks, beveled engine hood indicating twin-turbo 265H engine.

SD89MAC
- Prototype only.
- Isolated cab similar to SD90MAC-H II.
- Dual exhaust stacks, beveled engine hood indicating twin-turbo 265H engine.

The horsepower race reached a fever pitch in the early to mid-1990s as GM and GE clamored to be first with a 6000-h.p. A.C. traction locomotive. So intense was the competition that both builders took extraordinary measures, cataloging—and taking orders for—6000-h.p. models while the designs were still on the drawing board. The fact that neither builder had an existing engine capable of being upgraded to 6000 h.p. didn't seem to matter. Indeed, Union Pacific committed to EMD's 6000-h.p. SD90MAC while the model was little more than a concept.

Development of an all-new prime mover capable of producing 6000 h.p. gave Electro-Motive, a stalwart champion of two-cycle power since the early 1930s, its first production, four-cycle engine: the 16-cylinder, 265mm-bore, 300mm-stroke GM-16V265H. The power plant for the highly anticipated SD90MAC, the 265H evolved from concept to completion in a remarkable 18 months.

Showing off the redesigned carbody, with large radiators and the dynamic brake compartment at the rear of the hood, UP 8000, the first SD90MAC, works out on GMD's London, Ont., test track with BN SD70MAC 9679 on October 30, 1995. UP has a fleet of 309 upgradable SD90MAC's, classed by the railroad as SD9043AC.

However, teething pains with the new prime mover bogged the project down. Rather than delay the SD90MAC indefinitely, EMD struck an unprecedented compromise. The first SD90MAC's would be built with 4300-h.p. 16-710G3 engines and repowered and upgraded with the 6000-h.p. 265H when the new engine was put into production. Enter the "SD9043AC."

Externally identical to the SD80MAC, the 710-powered SD90MAC is basically an A.C. version of the SD75I. Intended—originally, at least—to be a temporary configuration, the 710-engined SD90MAC was given no specific model designation to differentiate it from the "real" SD90MAC, which EMD continued to market as a 6000-h.p., 265H-engined locomotive. To help eliminate the confusion, UP dubbed its 4300-h.p., 710-engine SD90MAC's "SD9043AC." As delays in H-engine production dragged on, and more and more 710-powered SD90MAC's hit the road, it became apparent that few—if any—units would be upgraded to 6000 h.p. and the SD9043AC was here to stay.

For a temporary model, the SD9043AC has fared relatively well, selling a total of 410 units to date. Union Pacific has thus far assembled a fleet of 309 "upgradable" SD90MAC's. The only other railroad to order the model so far has been Canadian Pacific, with 61 units—42 of which were assembled at the road's Ogden Shop in Calgary, Alberta. Rounding out the 710-powered SD90MAC population are 40 maroon

Canadian Pacific, the second railroad to order 4300-h.p., convertibles, assembled and painted 42 of its 61 SD90MAC's at its Ogden Shops in Calgary, Alta., in 1998-99. On August 22, 2000, Ogden-built CP SD90MAC's 9156 and 9148 lead westbound train 457 through Keppel, Sask. In addition to the UP and CP fleets, CIT Financial's 40 maroon and gray lease units, lettered CEFX 100-139, are the only other upgradable SD90MAC's built.

and gray CEFX units built for the lease fleet of CIT Financial. Not coincidentally, these units have spent most of their time on lease to UP and CP and are frequently employed in pool service between the two roads.

The long-awaited H-engine made its debut in September 1996 as EMD displayed UP 8160, the first of eight preproduction, 6000-h.p.

SD90MAC's, at the Railway Supply Association show in Chicago. Dual exhaust stacks of the twin-turbo 265H engine and the beveled edges of the engine compartment differentiate the 6000-h.p. SD90MAC from its 710-powered, upgradable kin. However, the most dramatic distinction is the gruff bark of the four-stroke 265H engine, a sound unlike that of any other EMD engine ever.

The preproduction units, including 8204 dressed in a special paint scheme to commemorate EMD's 75th anniversary, were put through rigorous tests at La Grange and the DOT test facilities at Pueblo, Colorado, as well as making shakedown runs on UP. In the spring of 1998, the first production-model 6000-h.p. SD90MAC's made their appearance as GMD London and Super Steel Schenectady began outshopping UP 8508-8521. With "SD90MAC-H" stamped on their builder's plates, the units were identical to their preproduction sisters (renumbered UP 8500-8507) and incorporated modifications and design improvements gleaned from experience with the testbeds. Despite the exhaustive preproduction trials, the entire UP SD90MAC-H fleet was plagued with teething pains and the units were frequently sidelined for modifications—sometimes for months at a time.

Still seeking to perfect the design, London outshopped a pair of "Phase II" SD90MAC-H testbeds in June

To avoid confusion between upgradable SD90MAC's powered with the 4300-h.p., 710 engine and those built with the 6000-h.p., 265H engine, EMD has designated the 6000-h.p. units as SD90MAC-H. In the field, there is little chance of confusing the two models. As shown by Phase I UP SD90MAC-H 8509, near Caliente, Calif., on March 29, 2001, the H-engined model sports a distinctly different engine hood with beveled edges, along with the less obvious dual exhaust stacks of the 265H.

1998. Built to UP specs, but painted solid white and lettered GM90 and GM91, the SD90MAC-H II prototypes featured a number of internal refinements, including an improved version of the 265H engine. On the outside, there were more obvious changes: the number of radiator fans was reduced from three to two; and the boxy end of the rear hood, with the sandbox jutting out from the dynamic brake compartment, was restyled to a smoother design. Conversely, the face of the Phase II took on an awkward, boxy look as the cab and nose were reprofiled to accommodate rectangular windows and a redesigned nose incorporating a full-height front door.

In the summer and fall of 1999,

A jagged nose, reprofiled to accommodate a full-height front door, and a boxy cab outfitted with rectangular windows are the hallmarks of the SD90MAC-H II. The new look, which also included restyling the dynamic brake compartment with a smoother design, accompanied a host of internal refinements as EMD worked to perfect the SD90MAC. Solid-white testbeds GM90 and GM91, built in June 1998, were the first SD90MAC-H II's, followed by UP 8522-8561 built at London and Super Steel Schenectady in 1999. Built by Super Steel and painted at Alstom's Hornell, N.Y., shop, UP SD90MAC-H II's 8541 and 8542 await delivery at Hornell on September 1, 1999. *Andrew McDonnell*

London and Schenectady out-shopped UP SD90MAC-H II's 8522-8561, but the 40 units were held for several months awaiting design improvements. Modifications were made at VMV's Paducah, Ky., shop and delivery commenced in February 2000. Canadian Pacific, the only other road to receive

SD90MAC-H II's, cut its order back from 20 units to 4, which were built at London in late 1999 and shipped to Alstom in Montreal for completion.

Although the advent of the 6000-h.p. diesel was hailed as the next revolution in railroading, its success has been limited at best. While both builders work to perfect their

respective designs, railroads are pondering the future of these high-horsepower monsters and whether or not they are just too powerful and or too complicated for general service.

Looking much like SD90MAC-H II testbeds GM90 and GM91, a third solid-white testbed emerged from London in June 2000. Numbered GM92, the mysterious unit has kept a low profile, undergoing testing at La Grange and the AAR's Transportation Test Center near Pueblo, Colorado. GM has kept mum on the subject, but the unit is reportedly equipped with a 12-cylinder version of EMD's 4-cycle 265H engine. The six-motor, A.C. locomotive is rated at 4500-h.p., and has, informally at least, been tagged an "SD89MAC." What ever its final designation may be, the new loco-motive would offer a four-cycle alter-native, if not replacement for EMD's 710-powered SD70MAC and go head-to-head with GE's eminently successful AC4400CW.

Built at London and completed by Alstom in Montreal, CP 9300-9303 are the only other SD90MAC-H II's built. Freshly polished for public display, CP 9302 poses at Calgary, Alta., on September 23, 2001.

Externally similar to SD90MAC-H II testbeds GM90 and GM91 is GM92, an EMD prototype equipped with a 12-cylinder version of the four-cycle 265H engine. Outshopped from London in June 2000, the unit has, unofficially at least, been dubbed an "SD89MAC." Engaged in high-altitude testing, GM92 is seen at Plain, Colo., on October 12, 2001. *Daren Genau*

The first F40PH of all, Amtrak 200 departs South Station in Boston, Mass., on March 2, 1978.

	F40PH	F40PH-2	F40PH-2M	F40PH-2C	F40PHM-2
Production Dates	1976-03 to 1988-02	1985-03 to 1989-10	1982-03, 1985-11	1987-07 to 1988-05	1991-10 to 1992-12
Total Built	325	90	4	26	30
Length	56'2"	56'2"	56'2"	64'3"	56'2"
Engine	16-645E3	16-645E3	16-645E3	16-645E3	16-645E3
Horsepower	3000/3200	3200	2000	3000	3200
Alternator	AR10	AR10	AR10	AR10	AR10
Traction Motors	D77	D77	D77	D77	D77
Weight x 1000 lb	260	260-268	266	282	265

F40PH
- Full-cowl carbody
- Early units have battery box and air reservoirs mounted ahead of fuel tank.
- Later units (1977 and after) have battery box and air reservoirs mounted behind fuel tank.

F40PH-2
- No major external differences.
- Battery box mounted ahead of fuel tank.

F40PH-2M
- Custom-built for Speno rail-grinding trains.
- Cab heavily modified—flush with front of unit.
- Two exhaust stacks, indicating normally aspirated 16-645E3 engine.

F40PH-2C
- Noticeably longer (8' 1") than F40PH, to accommodate Cummins HEP package.

F40PHM-2
- Full-cowl carbody, streamlined cab, built-out windshield sloping back from tip of nose.

An adaptation of the GP40-2, with a full-cowl carbody, high-speed gearing and a head-end power generator, the F40PH was designed for short-haul intercity passenger and commuter service. True to form, the first F40PH's built were purchased for just that sort of duty. Delivered in the spring of 1976, Amtrak 200-229 were assigned to corridor service out of Boston, New Haven, Chicago, Seattle and Los Angeles. Amtrak's intention was to employ the F40PH in short-haul corridor service, while the SDP40F ruled long-distance trains. However, the big SDP's soon fell from grace, and the little F40PH was thrust to the forefront to serve, not only as the backbone of Amtrak's entire diesel locomotive fleet, but as North America's standard passenger locomotive.

Although the original F40PH model designation lacked the formal Dash 2 suffix, all F40's are in fact Dash 2's. EMD began using the F40PH-2 model designation in 1985, but other than increasing the horse-

Toronto area commuter agency GO Transit introduced the F40PH to Canada with the purchase of six London-built units in 1978. Just about a month old, GO 511 rests in Willowbrook yard on June 5, 1978. Replaced by F59PH's, all six were sold to Amtrak in 1990.

power rating from 3000 to 3200 h.p., there were no significant changes. The boost in horsepower was a nominal effort to reduce the parasitic load of the HEP generator, which draws its power directly from the prime mover and can reduce the horsepower available for traction by as much as 700 h.p., depending upon HEP demands. For this reason, some operators of older F40PH's,

notably Amtrak and Metra, uprated these units from 3000 to 3200 h.p.

Following Amtrak's initial 30-unit order, the F40PH was modified to better suit its new role as a long-distance hauler. The original 1500-gallon fuel tank was enlarged to 1800 gallons and the output of the HEP generator bumped from 500 to 800 kw. Over the next dozen years, Amtrak acquired a fleet of

The extra length of the F40PH-2C, extended 8 feet to accommodate a separate Cummins Diesel HEP package, is evident in MBTA 1052, at East Cambridge, Mass., on September 3, 1990. MBTA 1050-1075 are the only EMD-built F40PH-2C's. However, Morrison-Knudsen and its successors have marketed a nearly identical locomotive, also designated F40PH-2C. MBTA rosters 12 of the Boise-built copies, numbered 1025-1036.
Scott A. Hartley

210 F40PH's, 123 of which were built with prime movers, traction motors, main alternators and other components from trade-in SDP40F's.

While the F40 is best known for its phenomenal success as Amtrak's workhorse, the locomotive has also succeeded in its intended role as a commuter locomotive, serving agencies from coast to coast. Chicago's Regional Transit Authority (now known as Metra) purchased the first commuter-service F40PH's in 1977 and has since accumulated a fleet of 115 units in the F40PH family. Other commuter operators rostering F40PH's include Boston's Massachusetts Bay Transportation Authority, NJ Transit and San Francisco's Bay Area commuter hauler CalTrain.

North of the border, Toronto's GO Transit acquired 6 GMD-built F40PH's (since sold to Amtrak), while VIA Rail Canada replaced aging MLW and GMD cab units with 59 F40PH-2's (rated at 3000 h.p.) purchased between 1986 and 1989.

Since the F40PH/F40PH-2 prime mover provides power for the HEP generator, it is necessary for the 16-645E engine to operate at or near full throttle, whether the locomotive is moving or standing still, in order to provide the train with heat, air-conditioning and lighting. The disadvantages of this arrangement include noise, fuel consumption and engine wear, issues that Boston's MBTA

VIA F40PH-2 6401, one of 59 such units purchased by the Canadian rail passenger agency, leads a pair of LRC coaches on train No. 70 at Paris, Ont., on October 1, 1996.

sought to address when, in 1987-88, it commissioned EMD to build 26 F40PH-2C's with separate engine-generator sets for head-end power. The addition of a Cummins diesel HEP package added just over 8 feet to the length of the F40PH-2C, but the concept was successful enough for MBTA to requisition another dozen F40PH-2C copies from Morrison-Knudsen in 1991-93.

If imitation is, in fact, the most sincere form of flattery, the success of the F40PH-2C can be measured in the fact that Morrison-Knudsen/ Boise Locomotive have done a respectable trade building knock-offs, not only for MBTA but for

Custom-built for Speno Rail Services (now Pandrol Jackson), the F40PH-2M, powered by a 2000-h.p., non-turbocharged 16-645E engine and built without HEP equipment, is essentially a GP38-2 in a modified F40PH shell. Speno purchased four of the unusual units, two in March 1982 and two in November 1985, and customized them in its own shop to serve as power cars for the firm's rail-grinding trains. Speno RMS-1 leads a rail-grinding train on CP Rail near Ayr, Ont., on July 12, 1983.

California commuter operators CalTrain and Coaster as well as for Miami's Tri-Rail.

Rail maintenance contractor Speno Rail Services (now Pandrol Jackson) contracted EMD for an unusual F40PH-2 derivative. More like a GP38-2 in an F40PH shell, the so-called F40PH-2M was built without HEP equipment and powered by a 2000-h.p., non-turbocharged 16-645E engine. Speno took delivery of four such units, two in March 1982 and two in November 1985, and customized them in its own shop to serve as power cars for the firm's rail-grinding trains. The cabs of these units have been extensively modified and bear no resemblance to those of standard F40's.

EMD closed the book on F40PH production with a 30-unit F40PHM-2 order placed by Chicagoland commuter hauler Metra. With a streamlined cab and built-out windshield that slopes back from the tip of its nose, the F40PHM-2 resembles no other member of the F40 family, but mechanically, the 3200-h.p. machine is no different than a standard F40PH-2. Delivered between October 1991 and December 1992, the Metra units were partially assembled at London and shipped to La Grange for completion. Outshopped in December 1992, Metra 214 was not only the last F40PH, but the last locomotive built at La Grange.

The last F40's were 30 streamlined-cab F40PHM-2's built between October 1991 and December 1992 for Chicagoland commuter hauler Metra. Partially assembled at London and shipped to La Grange for completion, Metra 185-214 were the last locomotives built at La Grange. On August 29, 1992, Metra 185 leads a westbound commuter train out of Western Springs, Ill.

Designed in close cooperation with Ontario's Toronto-area commuter agency GO Transit, the F59PH differs radically from the F40PH, the locomotive that it was designed to replace. The full-cowl, 710-powered F59PH is equipped with a separate HEP engine-generator set, features a CN-design comfort cab with a three-piece windshield and sports platforms at both ends. GO F59PH 534 heads an evening commuter train at Stouffville, Ont., on June 11, 1992.

	F59PH	F59PHI
Production Dates	1988-05 to 1994-05	1994-08 to current
Total Built	72	74
Length	58'2"	58'7"
Engine	12-710G3B	12-710G3B-EC
Horsepower	3000	3000
Alternator	AR15/CA5	AR15/CA6
Traction Motors	D87B	D87BTR
Weight x 1000 lb	260	268

F59PH
- Full-cowl carbody; CN/GMD-style comfort cab.
- Front platform and nose-door access to cab.

F59PHI
- Full-cowl carbody; streamlined cab with fiberglass nose.
- Side skirts over fuel tank.
- Carbody panels and roof profile to blend with coaches.

The F59PH was commissioned by, and designed in close cooperation with, Ontario's Toronto-area commuter agency GO Transit. The concept of a 3000-h.p., passenger locomotive powered with a 12-cylinder 710G3 engine and an independent HEP engine-generator set housed in a full-cowl carbody with a CN-style comfort cab was the brainchild of GO Transit's operations division. EMD was initially reluctant to embrace the idea, but GO made a strong case for the concept, and GO 520, the first F59PH, rolled out of London in May 1988.

EMD's positive reception to customer input paid off as the F59PH has proven to be technologically and commercially successful. GO made good on its commitment to the model, replacing its entire fleet and covering expansion services with a total of 49 F59PH's. However, the Canadian-born F59 has proven to be an even bigger hit on the West Coast.

In Los Angeles, Metrolink ordered 17 F59PH's for the October 1992

For the October 1992 startup of its Los Angeles-area commuter services, southern California commuter hauler Metrolink ordered 17 F59PH's, followed by a half dozen more as ridership and route mileage expanded. With four GO Transit-design bilevels in tow, Metrolink F59PH 871 approaches Riverside, Calif., on November 4, 1998.

startup of its L.A. area commuter services and quickly ordered a half-dozen more as route-mileage expanded. Metrolink, however, was just the start. California was about to make the F59 its own.

In 1994, the California Department of Transportation ordered nine F59's for state-funded "Amtrak California" services. Unlike the boxy GO and Metrolink F59's, Amtrak-California 2001-2009 featured isolated cabs and

Originally designed for Amtrak-California, the so-called "California" styling of the F59PHI has become standard, not just in California, but throughout the continent. Part of Amtrak's second F59PHI order, Super Steel-built 457 wheels a train of bilevel "California cars" into Riverbank, Calif., with train No. 716, on March 12, 2000.

F59PHI has received mixed reviews, but the design has proved popular. Metrolink ordered 8 F59PHI's of its own, while further up the coast, Seattle's Sound Transit "Sounder" and Vancouver, B.C.'s Translink commuter services have opted for "California F59's." Amtrak, meanwhile, bolstered its California fleet with 21 F59PHI's, all but one of which were built by Super Steel Schenectady, in Glenville, N.Y. As an add-on to the order, the North Carolina Department of Transportation received a pair of F59PHI's for state-funded, Amtrak-operated Raleigh-Charlotte and Raleigh-Asheville passenger service. The most recent orders F59PHI order saw 7 units assembled by Alstom in Montreal for hometown commuter duty in the employ of the Agence Metropolitaine de Transport and six more for Amtrak-California.

Nearly 15 years after GO Transit came knocking on EMD's door with a good idea, the F59 remains in the catalog.

a streamlined carbody complete with side skirts, a bulbous nose and carbody panels designed to blend with bi-level "California cars" ordered for the same service. Behind the fabricated shroud, though, the F59PHI—or California F59, as its come to be known—is simply a stock F59 with an isolated cab.

The California styling of the

In its natural environment, Metrolink "California" F59PHI cruises through the palms at Riverside, Calif., on November 4, 1998.

Housed in a carbody similar to that of the F40PHM-2 built for Metra, the two F69PHAC testbeds can be distinguished from their commuter-hauling counterparts by the ventilation grilles for A.C. traction equipment at the rear of the unit. Engaged in revenue-service testing on Amtrak, No. 450 works through Caledonia, Wis., on May 2, 1992. *Greg Mross*

	F69PHAC
Production Dates	1989-06
Total Built	2
Length	58'2"
Engine	12-710G3
Horsepower	3000
Alternator	NOT AVAILABLE
Traction Motors	1TB2626
Weight x 1000 lb	264

F69PHAC
- Full-cowl carbody and streamlined cab, similar to F40PHM-2.
- Grilles for A.C. traction equipment at rear below radiators.

The first all-new A.C. traction locomotives in North America, EMD F69PHAC experimentals 450 and 451 emerged from La Grange in June 1989. Outfitted with Siemens A.C. traction equipment and powered by a 12-710G prime mover, the slope-faced units were put through exhaustive tests at the Department of Transportation's Pueblo, Colo., test facility prior to entering service as Amtrak 450-451 in the fall of 1990. Dressed in standard Amtrak paint, the EMD-owned units racked up thousands of miles in revenue passenger service, while providing EMD's A.C. traction program with volumes of invaluable test data and operating experience. The two experimentals returned to La Grange in 1991, but reappeared briefly in 1993 to pilot a train of German-built Inter-City Express passenger equipment on a nationwide demonstration tour.

Having served their purpose as testbeds for the A.C. program, the F69's were removed from service and languished at La Grange until being sold for parts in 1999.

Painted for sponsors Amtrak, Siemens and Electro-Motive, F69PHAC's 450 and 451 wheel a demonstrating European ICE train consist through Blasdell, N.Y., on August 13, 1993. The ICE train tour was the units' last working assignment. *William D. Miller*

DM30AC *Joe Greenstein*

	DE30AC	DM30AC
Production Dates	1997-06 to current	1998-06 to current
Total Built	23	18
Length	75'0"	75'0"
Engine	12N-710G3B-EC	12N-710G3B-EC
Horsepower	3000	3000
Alternator	TA12QBE	TA12QBE
Traction Motors	AC-1TB2624	AC-1TB2624
Weight x 1000 lb	294	294

Built at Super Steel Schenectady, Long Island's monocoque-carbodied DE30AC and its dual-mode counterpart, the DM30AC, are EMD's first production model A.C. traction passenger locomotives. One of 23 conventional DE30AC's (as indicated by the lack of truck-mounted third-rail pickup shoes) Long Island 409 pauses at Mineola, N.Y., on February 23, 1999, with train No. 506 to Oyster Bay. *Joe Greenstein*

DE30AC
• Stainless-steel, monocoque carbody.
• Bolsterless two-axle truck; disc brakes.

DM30AC
• Stainless-steel, monocoque carbody.
• Bolsterless two-axle truck; disc brakes.
• Dual-mode; pickup shoes for third-rail electric operation.

Custom-designed for the Long Island Railroad, the DE30AC and DM30AC are EMD's first production-model, A.C. traction passenger locomotives. Measuring 75 feet over the couplers—just 5 feet, 2 inches shorter than an SD90MAC—and riding bolsterless two-axle trucks with 44 inch wheels and disc brakes, the two models share a common carbody, with a streamlined nose formed of a vinyl ester glass-fiber composite, a monocoque frame and stainless-steel shell. However, the DE30AC is a conventional diesel-electric, A.C. locomotive, while the DM30AC is a dual-mode locomotive capable of operating under its own diesel power or employing electric current drawn from the energized third rail in LIRR's electrified territory. This gives the DM30AC the ability to operate in the electric-only zone, specifically, through the East River Tunnel to Penn Station in New York. For New York-bound LIRR passengers on diesel-powered trains, the DM30AC means a one-seat trip into Penn

Third-rail pickup shoes mounted on the bolsterless trucks of Long Island 509, at Long Island City, N.Y., on February 10, 2000, identify the unit as one of 18 dual-mode DM30AC's capable of operating under its own diesel power or by drawing electric current from the energized third rail in LIRR's electrified territory.
Joe Greenstein

Station without changing trains at Jamaica.

Assembled by Super Steel Schenectady in Glenville, N.Y., a facility that owes its existence to the New York content requirement in the Long Island contract, the first DE30AC's were completed in June 1997; the first DM30AC's began rolling off the line a year later.

The road's first true passenger locomotives in decades, Long Island embraced the DE and DM30AC's with enthusiasm and high expectations. However, the units were soon plagued with failures, fires and structural cracks. EMD worked to resolve the problems, but not before the media got hold of the story and put the misfortunes of the DE's and DM's in the spotlight.

Morrison-Knudsen, now Wabtec subsidiary MotivePower Industries, has done a respectable trade remanufacturing and manufacturing locomotives for more than three decades. Included among the new locomotives built at Boise are a number of F40PH-2C's, based on the EMD locomotive of the same designation. On March 25, 1997, Boise-built San Diego Northern "Coaster" F40PH-2C 2105 heads through Leucadia, Calif.,with a San Diego-bound commuter train.

MotivePower Industries • Wabtec

A subsidiary of Wabtec, MotivePower Industries, of Boise, Idaho, traces its roots to Boise-based heavy construction and equipment contractor Morrison-Knudsen. Locomotives were no strangers to M-K, whose business often involved major railroad construction contracts that required the use of work trains. Having maintained and even rebuilt locomotives for its own use on some larger jobs, M-K broadened its business to include contract locomotive rebuilding in the early 1970s.

Heavy remanufacturing and upgrading was an M-K specialty, and the Boise shop performed from-the-rails-up rebuilds of hundreds of locomotives, from BN's fleet of Chicago commuter E9's to the D&H PA's and Conrail Geeps. In some cases, M-K

Caterpillar-powered Port Terminal MK1500D's 9626 and 9629 switch at Houston, Texas, on March 22, 1998.
J. David Ingles

even created its own unique-looking rebuilds, combining the frame and trucks from one builder's locomotive with the prime mover and other components of another—all housed in a Boise-built carbody.

In an attempt to expand its locomotive business and develop a North American market for Swiss-design Sulzer diesel engines, M-K

197

M-K builder's plate, San Diego Northern, Coaster F40PH-2C 2102.

engaged in several experimental repowering programs. Between 1978 and 1982, Sulzer diesels were installed in quartets of Southern Pacific U25B's and Santa Fe SD45's, as well as a half-dozen Union Pacific SD45's and a single ex-UP GP9 demonstrator. The Sulzer experiment lasted just a few years, and with the exception of MK 5001, the Geep demonstrator, all of the testbeds were retired or repowered by 1987.

M-K, meanwhile, found its niche transforming GP40's into HEP-equipped commuter locomotives designed to offer alternatives to the EMD F40PH. Although built on the frames of old GP40's, many of the rebuilds bore little if any resemblance to their old selves. Mechanically, they were the next thing to new locomotives. Some had cowl carbodies mated with the GP40 cab, while others were near clones of the F40PH, with cabs and carbodies from retired F45's grafted onto the GP40 frame.

But for the reuse of frames, trucks and a few other components, many M-K rebuilds were virtually new locomotives. Considering the scope of the Boise shop's remanufacturing process, graduation to the construction of completely new locomotives was a natural move. In 1991, M-K began doing just that.

Nine Massachusetts Bay Transportation Authority F40PH-2C's built for Boston-area commuter service in 1991 were M-K's first "new" locomotives. Almost identical to the EMD model of the same designation, the units did incorporate some remanufactured components, such as trucks, traction motors and alternators, but are nevertheless considered new locomotives.

Throughout the 1990s, corporate restructuring changed the banner under which the Boise shop operated—from Morrison-Knudsen to M-K Rail in 1994, and to the Boise Locomotive Co., a subsidiary of MotivePower Industries, in 1997. MotivePower then became a division of Wilmerding, Pa., based Wabtec. Under the M-K and MPI flag, the company broadened its operations to include a large lease fleet of rebuilt locomotives, and for a short time operated satellite rebuild shops at Hornell, N.Y., and Mountain Top, Pa.

The cornerstone of the M-K/BLC/MPI operations throughout years of corporate change, the Boise shop expanded its line of new locomotives to include not only the F40PH-2C, but the microprocessor-equipped F40PH-3C, as well as a series of Caterpillar-engined switchers and a half-dozen 5000-h.p., Caterpillar-powered MK5000C fielded as demonstrators for a still-born line of road-freight locomotives.

While total production figures for the M-K/BLC/MPI line of locomotives are low in comparison to those of GE and EMD, Boise-built units have found homes throughout the country. Although its proposed line of road locomotives went no further than the testbed-demonstrators, Boise continues to build F40PH knock-offs for commuter agencies, as well as

The high-visibility cab of BNSF 1201, a natural-gas-powered MK1200G, contrasts with that of Santa Fe CF7 rebuild 2619 on the Los Angeles Junction Railway on March 31, 2001.

Caterpillar-powered switchers.

In 1998, Electro-Motive, Caterpillar and MotivePower Industries formed a unique alliance to market a refined version of MPI's Caterpillar-powered MP1500D and MP2000D switchers

as EMD GP15D and GP20D models. Under the EMD label, just 50 of the high-cabbed, pug-nosed units have sold—25 GP15D's and 25 GP20D's to lease-fleet operator CIT Financial.

Relettered BNSF and assigned to the Los Angeles Junction Railway, natural-gas-fueled MK1200G's 1201 and 1200 mingle with LAJ CF7's at the road's shop on March 31, 2001. The units' heavily insulated cylindrical LNG fuel tanks distinguish the natural-gas-powered MK1200G from its conventional diesel-fueled counterparts, the MK1500D and MP1500D.

MK1200G
- Built on frame and remanufactured Blomberg trucks of retired EMD GP7/GP9.
- Sloping pug nose; tall cab with expansive windows on all sides.
- Low-profile engine hood; single exhaust stack; two radiator fans.
- Heavily insulated cylindrical fuel tanks designed keep 1400 gallons of LNG at minus 260 degrees Fahrenheit.

MK1500D/MP1500D
- Similar to MK1200G, but with standard EMD-style diesel fuel tank.

MP2000D
- Similar to MK1500D/MP1500D, but built on longer frame.
- First demonstrator built on GP35 frame; rest on new frames.

MP2000C
- Built on frame and remanufactured C-C Flexicoil trucks of retired EMD SD.
- Carbody similar to MK/MP 1500D, etc., with sloping pug nose and tall cab with expansive windows on all sides. Low-profile engine hood; single exhaust stack; two radiator fans.
- MPEX 6201 only unit built.

	MK1200G	MK1500D	MP1500D	MP2000D	MP2000C
Production Dates	1993-11 to 1994-06	1996-06 to 1996-12	1997-05 to 1999-03	1997-08 to 1999-06	1998-09
Total Built	4	32	6	7	1
Length	56'2"	56'2"	56'2"	57'2"	60'8"
Engine	CAT 3516NG	CAT 3512A	CAT 3512A	CAT 3516A	CAT 3516
Horsepower	1200	1380-1400	1400	1963	1963
Alternator	KATO 8P6.5-3000	KATO 8P6.5-3000	KATO 8P6.5-3000	KATO 8P6.5-3400	KATO 8P6.5-3400
Traction Motors	EMD D78B	EMD D78B	D78B	D87B	D87B
Weight x 1000 lb	250	256	256	260	385

Morrison-Knudsen broke new ground with the construction of four natural-gas-powered MK1200G switchers in 1993-94. Assigned to Los Angeles, Calif., Union Pacific 1298-1299 and Santa Fe 1200-1201 were the first new LNG-fueled locomotives in North America.

Although built with the frames, remanufactured trucks and traction motors of retired EMD Geeps, the pug-nosed, high-cabbed switchers can hardly be considered rebuilds. In fact, the MK1200G, with its M-K designed microprocessor controls and turbocharged, four-stroke, Caterpillar 3516 diesel—modified to burn liquid natural gas—ranks as the first third-generation yard and transfer locomotive in North America.

The MK1200G's performed satisfactorily, but no further orders were received for the LNG-powered switcher. However, M-K offered the same basic locomotive in a standard diesel-powered configuration designated the MK1500D. With a Caterpillar 3512 series engine rated

Assigned to Los Angeles, Calif., Union Pacific 1298-1299 and Santa Fe 1200-1201 were the first new LNG-fueled locomotives in North America. Sandwiched between EMD SW1500's, UP 1299 rests at Spence St. in Los Angeles, on November 27, 1997.

at 1400 h.p., the MK1500D appears almost identical to the MK1200G, fuel tanks providing the only major outward distinction between the two models. The MK1200G is outfitted with heavily insulated cylindrical tanks designed to keep its 1400 gallons of LNG at minus 260 degrees Fahrenheit, while the MK1500D features a standard EMD-style fuel tank.

Texas terminal-switching roads Houston Belt & Terminal and the Port Terminal Railroad purchased 32 MK1500D's before the model designation was changed to MP1500D to reflect the change from Morrison-Knudsen to MotivePower Industries in 1997. Essentially identical to its MK predecessor, the MP1500D sold only six units before being superceded by the EMD/BLC GP15D.

At Houston Texas., on March 22, 1998, Port Terminal Railroad MK1500D 9630 exhibits the hallmark look of Boise-built switcher/road-switchers: a high-visibility cab and low-profile engine hood—with the single exhaust stack of the Caterpillar diesel and two radiator fans—all on the frame and Blomberg trucks of an EMD Geep. In 1997, the model designation was changed to MP1500D. MotivePower also builds a modified version of this locomotive for EMD, which is marketed as the GP15D. *J. David Ingles*

In 1997, Boise Locomotive bolstered its line of Caterpillar-powered switchers with the 1963-h.p. MP2000D. The first unit, demonstrator 2001, was constructed on the frame of a retired GP35, but subsequent units were built on new platforms. Only seven MP2000D's, five of them demonstrators, were built before the model was replaced by the EMD/BLC GP20D.

Boise Locomotive rounded out its Caterpillar-engined, MP series switcher/road-switcher line with the six-axle MP2000C, introduced in 1998. Built on the frame and remanufactured trucks of an SP SD35, the MP2000C featured the same high-mounted cab and low-profile carbody employed by its four-axle counterparts. Demonstrator 6201, thus far the only MP2000C built, was outshopped in September 1998 and has worked on a number of roads in the United States and Canada. However, no orders have yet been placed for the Caterpillar-powered C-C.

Bearing a strong resemblance to the MK1500D and MP1500D, but built on the frame of a retired EMD GP35, primer-painted MP2000D prototype 2001 tests near Boise, Idaho, with Boise-rebuilt Helm SD's and an MK5000C in June 1997. Subsequent MP2000D's (only six more have been built) have been constructed on new frames. The EMD GP20D, which MotivePower also builds, is a modified version of the MP2000D, built in Boise, but marketed by Electro-Motive.
Keith E. Ardinger

Built on the frame of retired SP SD35 2958, Caterpillar-powered, Boise Locomotive demonstrator MPEX 6201, at Boise, Idaho, on August 16, 1998, is the only MP2000C built to date. *Keith E. Ardinger*

Outshopped from Boise in 1994, the three Phase I MK5000C demonstrators were dressed in Southern Pacific paint and numbered SP 501-503. Returned to the builder, the demos operated sporadically as lease units until being sold to the Utah Railway in 2001. In between assignments, SP 501 and 502 stand idle at Mid-America Car in Kansas City, Mo., November 13, 1999.
Robert E. Lambrecht

	MK5000C PHASE I	MK5000C PHASE II
Production Dates	1994-03 to 1994-06	1995-08
Total Built	3	3
Length	71'2"	73'4"
Engine	CAT 3612	CAT 3612
Horsepower	5000	5000
Alternator	KATO TA16SL	KATO TA16SL
Traction Motors	MK1000	MK1000
Weight x 1000 lb	390-420	390-420

MK5000C (Phase I)
- M-K version of North American cab, with angular, sloping nose and centered, full-height nose door.
- Tall engine hood, four radiator fans.
- MLW-design Dofasco trucks; EMD-style fuel tank.

MK5000C (Phase II)
- Built on longer frame.
- Larger end-platforms with five access steps vs four on Phase I.
- Otherwise similar to Phase I MK5000C.

The crown jewel in M-K's planned line of Caterpillar-powered road locomotives was to be the 5000-h.p., microprocessor-equipped MK5000C. Featuring M-K's version of the North American cab, with an angular, sloping nose and centered, full-height nose door, a tall engine hood, four cooling fans and Dofasco high-adhesion trucks similar to those used by MLW, the MK5000C resembled nothing else on the road.

Three demonstrators painted Southern Pacific 501-503 were dispatched from Boise in mid-1994, followed by three M-K painted demos released in the summer of 1995 and assigned to Union Pacific. The two sets of demos were basically similar, with the exception of a stepped increase in the length of the Phase II units, along with a change from four to five steps at both ends.

In early 1996, the locomotives returned to Boise, having generated no orders. They saw sporadic service as lease units before becoming Utah Railway 5001-5006 in 2001.

Slightly longer than the Phase I prototypes, Phase II MK5000C's 9901-9903, built for demonstration on Union Pacific, can be identified by the larger end-platforms, along with the presence of five, rather than four steps. Demonstrating on UP, MK5000C 9902 is coupled to a UP SD60 at Yermo, Calif., on December 10, 1995.
Paul Wester, Mark R. Lynn collection

A small air intake behind the last set of radiator grilles is the only external feature distinguishing the Boise-built F40PH-2C and the EMD model of the same designation. On Coaster F40PH-2C 2102, built by M-K Boise in August 1994, this feature appears in the form of two small sets of louvers just above the white stripe at the very rear of the carbody. Awaiting the startup of North County Transit's Coaster commuter service to San Diego, F40PH-2C 2102 rests at Oceanside, Calif., on November 23, 1994.

	F40PH-2C	F40PH-3C
Production Dates	1991-05 to 1998-12	1994-07 to current
Total Built	23	5
Length	64′3″	64′3″
Engine	16-645E	16-645E
Horsepower	3000	3200
Alternator	AR10/D14	AR10/D14
Traction Motors	D78B	D78B
Weight x 1000 lb	282	277

F40PH-2C (M-K/Boise Locomotive version)
- Full-cowl carbody, externally identical to EMD F40PH-2C, but for small air-intake behind last set of radiator grilles.

F40PH-3C
- Outwardly identical to M-K/Boise Locomotive F40PH-2C.

The F40PH-2C, with its separate engine-generator set for HEP generation, was first commissioned by the Massachusetts Bay Transportation Authority in an effort to reduce noise, fuel consumption and engine wear. EMD built 26 F40PH-2C's for the Boston commuter agency in 1987-88, but when the MBTA wanted more, it turned to Morrison-Knudsen for exact copies.

After nearly 20 years in the locomotive rebuilding business, M-K graduated to a bonafide locomotive builder with the MBTA's 1991 order for nine F40PH-2C's. Inside and out, the M-K F40PH-2C's are almost identical to the EMD model of the same designation, although Boise used some remanufactured parts, including trucks, traction motors, alternators and engine components in its units. The only significant external difference between the EMD and M-K versions of the F40PH-2C is the presence of a small air-intake just behind the last set of radiator grilles at the rear of the Boise-built units.

Motive Power's latest passenger locomotive is the microprocessor-equipped successor to the F40PH-2C, the externally identical F40PH-3C. One of five F40PH-3C's built for California's Altamont Commuter Express, ACE 3104 works in push mode along the southern shores of San Francisco Bay, north of Alviso, Calif., with San Jose to Stockton No. 2 on March 14, 2001. *Vic Neves*

Following the MBTA order, Boise adopted the F40PH-2C as its own, constructing a second group for the Boston agency, as well as additional units for Miami's Tri-Rail and for California commuter operators CalTrain and North County Transit's San Diego-area "Coaster" service.

In 1997, Boise Locomotive applied third-generation technology to the F40PH-2C to produce a new, upgraded version of its standard commuter locomotive. Outwardly identical to the F40PH-2C, the F40PH-3C is equipped with microprocessor controls and boasts improved adhesion and wheel-slip control, along with increased fuel efficiency and a higher, 3200-h.p. rating. For the 1998 startup of its 82-mile, Stockton-San Jose service, California's Altamont Commuter Express purchased three F40PH-3C's in late 1997 and took delivery of two more in August 2000. The five ACE units are thus far the only F40PH-3's built.

Index

TRAINS Magazine: Your Best Resource For Railroading Information!

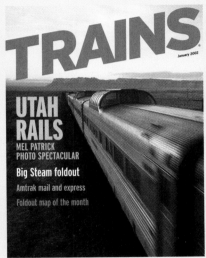

UTAH RAILS
MEL PATRICK
PHOTO SPECTACULAR

Big Steam foldout

Amtrak mail and express

Foldout map of the month

$39.95
12 issues/year
$50.00 Canadian/foreign

- Latest news of railroads including locomotives, passenger, rail transit, and museums and excursions

- Detailed maps of railroads current and historic

- In-depth analysis and insight on railroads today

- Technology, history, and operation of railroads

- Spectacular photographs from the best photographers

Start Your Subscription Today!

[X] **YES!** Send me one year (12 issues) of TRAINS for only $39.95. I'll **save 32%** off the annual newsstand rate!

Name_____

Address_____

City_____

State_____ Zip_____

Country_____

Canadian price $50.00 (GST included, payable in U.S. funds). Foreign price $50.00 (payable in U.S. funds, checks must be drawn on a U.S. bank). Make checks payable to Kalmbach Publishing Co.

T39353IN   L181T1

TRAINS MAGAZINE

Your satisfaction is guaranteed!

If you're ever dissatisfied—for any reason—you may receive a refund on any unmailed issues.

To start your railroading adventure, mail this card today!

Your reliable railroading resource!

NO POSTAGE
NECESSARY
IF MAILED
IN THE
UNITED STATES

BUSINESS REPLY MAIL

FIRST-CLASS MAIL   PERMIT NO. 16   WAUKESHA, WI

POSTAGE WILL BE PAID BY ADDRESSEE

TRAINS

PO BOX 1612
WAUKESHA WI 53187-9950